D1353114

teach yourself

small business
health check

anna hipkiss

teach yourself
70
1938 2008
celebrate
with us

Launched in 1938, the **teach yourself** series grew rapidly in response to the world's wartime needs. Loved and trusted by over 50 million readers, the series has continued to respond to society's changing interests and passions and now, 70 years on, includes over 500 titles, from Arabic and Beekeeping to Yoga and Zulu. What would you like to learn?

be where you want to be with **teach yourself**

For UK order enquiries: please contact Bookpoint Ltd, 130 Milton Park, Abingdon, Oxon OX14 4SB. Telephone: +44 (0) 1235 827720. Fax: +44 (0) 1235 400454. Lines are open 09.00–17.00, Monday to Saturday, with a 24-hour message answering service. Details about our titles and how to order are available at www.teachyourself.co.uk

Long renowned as the authoritative source for self-guided learning – with more than 50 million copies sold worldwide – the **teach yourself** series includes over 500 titles in the fields of languages, crafts, hobbies, business, computing and education.

British Library Cataloguing in Publication Data: a catalogue record for this title is available from the British Library.

First published in UK 2005 by Hodder Education, part of Hachette Livre UK, 338 Euston Road, London, NW1 3BH.

This edition published 2005.

The **teach yourself** name is a registered trade mark of Hodder Headline.

Typeset by Transet Limited, Coventry, England.
Printed in Great Britain for Hodder Education, an Hachette Livre UK Company, 338 Euston Road, London NW1 3BH, by CPI Cox & Wyman, Reading, Berkshire, RG1 8EX.

The publisher has used its best endeavours to ensure that the URLs for external websites referred to in this book are correct and active at the time of going to press. However, the publisher and the author have no responsibility for the websites and can make no guarantee that a site will remain live or that the content will remain relevant, decent or appropriate.

Hachette Livre UK's policy is to use papers that are natural, renewable and recyclable products and made from wood grown in sustainable forests. The logging and manufacturing processes are expected to conform to the environmental regulations of the country of origin.

Impression number   10 9 8 7 6 5 4 3 2
Year   2012 2011 2010 2009 2008

contents

This book is written for anyone who is running an established small business. The business can be of any type – a shop or café, a consultancy or a factory – the tactics for success are pretty similar, and you can be sure of finding material relevant to your own operation in this book. The business may have been running for 18 months or 5 years – but you are well past the start-up phase.

'Small' is not defined in terms of staff or sales – it is any operation from one person upwards. What defines 'small' is that you, the person running it, can 'put your arms around it' and feel that it is yours. You might do that with 50 staff, or with none, the point is that the running of the business is still in your hands.

You know that many small businesses fail for a number of classic reasons, and you want to make sure that you do not make those mistakes. You also want to know the success factors, so that you can take those on board, and make your business whatever you want it to be – bigger and better, small and secure – however you define success. This book will help you to clarify what success means to you.

In this book, you will learn from many real-life experiences how and why businesses go wrong, how to avoid the pitfalls altogether, or how to survive when disaster hits. You will also learn, from a different set of real-life experiences, what makes small businesses successful, and how you can incorporate those tactics for success into your own business.

This is not a technical book; we will not be exploring the intricacies of cash flow forecasting or inventory control. It may be that your business needs such specialist expertise, but this book will give you the basics, to enable you to recognize what you need, and help you to find 'a man who can'.

The reality is that most of the elements of success are already in your hands, but you may not be aware of them all yet. By the end of this book, you will know what they are, and how to use them.

Acknowledgements

Thank you to all those small businesses who shared their stories with me, some of you chose to be anonymous, but you know who you are! Others were happy for me to use their real names, so many thanks go to:

Steve Feigen of Abacus E-media, www.abacusemedia.com (Chapter 2); Alastair Bathgate of Blue Prism, www.blueprism.co.uk (Chapter 26); Ben Ritson of Domane Interiors, www.domaneinteriors.com (Chapter 5); Henry Stewart of Happy Computers, www.happy.co.uk (Chapter 20).

Other key contributors to the book include:

Mike Cheeseman, who provided an invaluable investor's perspective; Karyn Bright of E-Co and Alan Ford of IBD – both of whom helped me to gather case study material; Graham Jenner, who cast a financial eye over the appropriate chapters. I also received helpful feedback on various sections of the book from Kate Dann, Chris Dodd, Dave Edwards, Bill Pougher and Polly Simpson, plus ideas on the cash flow diagrams from Dave Suttle.

Thanks also to friends and family, who helped me to find the right small businesses to talk to, and to my husband, Richard, for his unfailing support, in every sense of the word.

The publishers would like to thank the following for permission to reproduce copyright material: Figures 2, 3, 5 and 6 on pp. 106, 107, 110, 122: reproduced with the kind permission of Bizled, Institute for Learning and Research Technology, University of Bristol, www.bizled.co.uk, 'Stable Cash Flow'.

Every effort has been made to trace all copyright holders, but if any have been inadvertently overlooked the Publishers will be pleased to make the necessary arrangements at the first opportunity.

Disclaimer

I have gone to great lengths to use real case study material in this book, and some companies were happy for me to use their real names. Others were not, and so I have gone to equal lengths to disguise the companies and the people involved, to protect everyone's confidentiality. If, in creating these disguises, I have used names which you recognize, this is unfortunate because, as they say at the beginning of all the best books, all the names I have used are fictional. Any resemblance to real people or companies is purely coincidental.

About the author

Anna Hipkiss has broad experience of running large and small businesses. She has been a director and general manager of businesses in diverse industries, including consumer goods and computer software. She has experience of manufacturing, retailing and service operations. She has set up small businesses with her partner which have flourished over many years, but not without problems and adversity along the way.

This book is therefore written not from textbook theory, but from the realities of Anna's personal experience of the road to success.

Anna is now a business consultant, and can be contacted via www.solutionsinwriting.co.uk

There are a number of ways in which you can use this book and, before you dive in, you will find it helpful to understand how it is structured, so that you can find what you want quickly and easily.

Introduction

Here, the processes that a company doctor would follow with a company in trouble are described, so that you can apply this tool – the company doctor diagnosis kit – to the companies in Part 1, and then to your own situation.

Part 1 – diagnosis

One of the biggest challenges for small business owners is to diagnose their own problems. You may think that selling is the issue, when it is really your market analysis which is letting you down. You may blame the economy instead of your poor customer service. To help you to make a diagnosis, the first ten chapters in the book describe the major reasons why businesses fail. Each one tells the story of a real company that suffered, went to the brink and, in most cases, managed to recover. Each business owner then describes the lessons they have learned from their experience, and finally the company doctor identifies the success tactics which will avoid the problem altogether. The real names of the company doctors have been changed in this book.

The success tactics relate to the specifics of each pitfall, but most of them are common to more than one pitfall. Flexibility in business structure, for example, is a success tactic in avoiding five of the ten pitfalls.

Part 2 – solutions

Chapters 11 to 22 cover the key success tactics that are crucial to small business success. Part 1 tells you what they are, and where they have real impact; Part 2 tells you how to put them into practice. For example, in Chapter 2 you will read about the company that ran out of cash, and how the flexibility of business structure impacts on cash flow. When you come to Chapter 19, which is dedicated to that tactic, it will tell you how to create flexibility in your business structure, and what it does for your business overall, not just in relation to cash.

Part 3 – moving on

Chapters 23 to 27 deal with the next step: how to move your business forward and how to define success for you, which may or may not mean growth. This part of the book builds on all the material from the success tactics, and results in a very natural, forward-looking conclusion.

This structure enables you to approach the book in three ways:

1 You can set out to diagnose a problem that you are sure you currently have, such as low sales, and read the relevant chapters in Part 1, with the related success tactics from Part 2.

2 You can read the book in sequence – although it can be dipped into, it also stands as a complete work.

3 If you are looking only at future development, you might wish to skip some of the pitfalls in Part 1 and read the rest of the book in sequence – the success tactics in Part 2 are the foundation for Part 3. For example, the essentials of marketing are covered in Part 2, and they serve as the foundation for the marketing plans you will be making in Part 3 to develop or change your business.

diagnostic kit

Diagnose your company's strengths and weaknesses, opportunities and threats

'Physician, heal thyself' is a well-known expression which highlights how difficult it is for doctors to recognize and treat their own illnesses, and it has many parallels in other fields. It can be difficult to apply your own expertise to yourself because you do not see yourself objectively, and therefore cannot produce an independent diagnosis. This is exactly the problem that many small businesses face. They know that things are not right, but they are not sure precisely which things are causing the problem. Often, they will have found what they think is the real issue, only to discover when they fix it that it was not the problem after all.

Normally, a Teach Yourself® book would dive straight in, and tell you how to speak Japanese or play golf. With small businesses, it is far less obvious what problem to solve so there is no point in teaching you cash management if your problem turns out to be marketing. Part 1 of this book is therefore about problem diagnosis – helping you to decide if you need to teach yourself about marketing or finance or something else entirely. This is done through a variety of real small business case histories, describing the different mistakes that they made, and how, in most cases, they managed to recover. When you read about these companies, you will be able to recognize any problems you share with them, and when you have identified your own problem, you can go to Part 2 for the solution.

Before we come to the case histories, this section covers the process a company doctor would go through with each case so that you can apply the methodology yourself and conduct a more thorough diagnosis of the current state of your business and its potential.

Small business company doctor

Let us imagine that you have been asked to become a company doctor for a small mail order business called S&B Knits that has been running for six years, selling knitwear. Shirley and Brenda set it up from their living room, and they source most of their products from companies in Scotland and Italy. Over time, they have taken on five staff, all part-time, and moved to small office premises nearby. They have called you in because the business seems to have stalled. Sales are completely flat, and have been for the past 18 months. 'We just aren't growing any more,' Shirley tells you, 'and we can't work out why, because we are targeting new customers all the time.'

Sales or marketing problems would seem to be the obvious place to look, but being a good doctor, you do a thorough examination, and do not leap to conclusions. You will therefore work through the following steps:

1 Interview the two owners carefully to understand how the business is run and what their priorities and goals are.

2 Examine the accounts to get a financial feel for the business.

3 The company has no debt and no investors other than the owners so there is no further work to do in this area, but you will wish to talk to their accountant.

4 As there are only five other staff, you can talk to them all and obtain a view of what they do and what they think is happening in the business. Often, even the most junior staff know a great deal about the way a company works, but people rarely bother to ask them.

5 As you talk to the staff, you will walk around the company premises, looking at equipment, stock, and getting a feel for the place. From all this, you will form a clear view of how the company operates and its key business processes, which will include sales, marketing and buying.

6 Next, you will study the customer data and talk to a cross-section of clients, happy and unhappy. You will look at rates of return, and find out first hand what customers think.

7 Talk to the company's key suppliers and find out their view of this particular client. Apart from the company's product suppliers, this will also include the company that creates their catalogue and does their mailings.

You have the advantage in doing all this of being well out of the trees, and you can clearly see the woods. Being independent, you can have frank conversations with everyone involved and bring a completely fresh approach, which is difficult for Shirley or Brenda to do. So what do you find?

1 The owners are hard working and committed. They run the business efficiently and are focused on delivering a quality product at a good price to their customers. They believe they know their market and they are not interested in what the competition are doing.

2 Finance is becoming problematic. Profit margins are narrow and, although present sales are able to sustain the company cost base, any decline in sales will take the company into loss quite quickly.

3 The accountant confirms this view, although he has not pointed this out to his clients as he thinks it is obvious from the numbers he provides them.

4 Staff are clear on their roles and carry them out efficiently. They were surprised to be asked about the business. Helen, who deals with the returns, said that returns were decreasing since they were careful to tighten up on any problem that was identified, such as inaccurate colours in the brochure or size variations. Jo, who takes telephone orders, said that a few customers had remarked that they already had most of the stuff in the brochure, and she wondered if they needed to introduce more variety. She had not mentioned this to anyone else until now.

5 Business processes impress you. Clearly much has been invested in a good computer system, and the whole operation runs like the proverbial tight ship.

6 Analysis of the customer data is revealing. It shows a loyal client base with a slowly declining reorder rate, and a regular flow of new customers, less than 5 per cent of whom reorder. You talk to a cross-section of all these types, and find that Jo is right:

'A lovely company, and I like their products, but I've got a few of them now and I don't see anything else that I need.'

7 'I bought a sweater and it was fine, but I haven't bought anything else because it's all pretty much the same.'

'I wish they'd do more colours. I like to have a wardrobe of basic sweaters, so I buy a new colour when it comes up, but they tend to go for muddy colours rather than bright ones, so I haven't got very many.'

8 Talking to knitwear suppliers reinforces this view: S&B buy a narrow range of products but are seen as a good customer, easy to deal with, they know what they want and pay promptly. The marketing agency is run by Marianne, a friend of Brenda's. Marianne tells you that the brochure has always been created on a tight budget, but to a good standard, and they do regular mailings to existing customers, and to new ones. She sources lists for them as close to their customer profile as possible. It does not take long to find out that although she is very experienced in brochure design, her direct marketing skills are not the strongest. She is not able to give you a clear view of the market or the competition.

Your recommendations

You are now in a position to report on your preliminary findings to Shirley and Brenda. The fact is that S&B Knits will soon go into decline unless they broaden their offering and target new customers more effectively.

Margin

You review the narrow margin and point out the impact of a sales decline, which they immediately recognize.

You raise the issue of improving margin – cutting operating costs does not seem an appropriate step in such an efficiently run organization. They keep stock levels low, but you question whether there is scope to renegotiate terms with their suppliers.

The other obvious route is to increase prices. You suggest researching what prices the competition are charging, and doing some price sensitivity testing, perhaps by introducing a new and more expensive line, to see if customers are willing to pay more.

Accountant

You are concerned that their accountant sees himself only as a number cruncher. You question whether the company needs more proactive financial advice.

Market research

You recommend that Shirley and Brenda find out from their regular customers what other products they are looking for, as a basis for broadening their range. You strongly suggest a thorough review of the competition, which they cannot afford to ignore. They can use their suppliers as another source of information.

Direct marketing
With the brochure that they will create for the new extended range, you propose a strong 'recommend a friend' incentive scheme, since existing customers are the best source of new ones in this case.

You also recommend some professional direct marketing advice, to help S&B Knits to target new customers more tightly.

Market intelligence
Finally, you point out to Shirley and Brenda that they are missing a key piece of market intelligence – their own staff – and advise that they gather input from staff on a systematic basis, either through informal chats or through holding a regular business ideas meeting.

Motivation
Holding a regular business ideas meeting (see above) will be highly motivating for the team, making them feel that their contribution is valued at a higher level, and encouraging them to gather intelligence more actively.

Conclusion
Although this issue looked like a marketing problem for S&B Knits, and proved to be one, it was still important to investigate all areas of the company since a number of other issues arose which could easily have been missed had the thorough diagnosis not been completed. In reality, many problems which look like one thing turn out to be quite another, which is why it is vital to gather information first hand, in every area and at every level. It can then be helpful to summarize it under four headings: your strengths and weaknesses, and the opportunities and threats that you face, as shown here for S&B Knits:

Strengths	Weaknesses
Clear business focus	Static product range
Efficient operation	Poor market awareness
Good staff	Lack of competitive information
Quality products	Inadequate marketing programme
Reliable service	Poor financial advice
Satisfied customer base	Low margin
Good supplier relations	
Opportunities	**Threats**
Build on good customer base	Changing market trends
Develop potential through	Competition
good marketing	Economic downturn
Diversify and extend	
product range	

Applying the diagnosis to your own company

To put some distance between you and your company, it is very helpful to enlist the help of others, ideally a small company doctor, who can be more affordable than you think (see 'Taking it further' at the back of the book for more information). As an alternative, if you have one or more business colleagues who could gather some information and give you a perspective that will be much better than you struggling to see the wood when you are actually standing among your own trees!

The above case study is deliberately simple since the focus is on the process of diagnosis rather than the company problem, but you can see that even with a straightforward situation like this one, there are still many ramifications in other areas. The biggest pitfall in diagnosis is to narrow down the solution too quickly.

When you find, among all the company dramas on the following pages, a problem (or problems) that matches your own, test it with your company doctor's diagnostic kit. When you have a match, you can move on to the easy bit – applying the solutions!

part 1

diagnosis: the top ten

reasons why small

businesses fail

01

costs too high

When your business takes off and you suddenly find that you are struggling to keep up with demand, it is easy to spend money to solve the problem. You hire more staff, you need bigger premises, and you may feel that your new premises should reflect the image of the successful company you have become.

You may also invest in projects to broaden your offering or to create your own products, which will eventually be more profitable than your current range. Eventually can be a long time – longer than you had planned – which is exactly what Jelonair found, and this was all seriously compounded by a personal problem in the partnership.

Company profile: Jelonair

Howard and Josh had worked together in a large multinational company for many years. The company produced a range of consumer products, and they both specialized in the cleaning sector. With backgrounds in chemistry and biochemistry, and experience in sales and marketing, Howard and Josh were experts in their field. One day, Howard came up with the idea of a specialist cleaning product for hospitals. They put a plan together and presented it to the product review board, and were desperately disappointed when it was turned down.

Howard and Josh decided to set up their own business and do it themselves. They formed a partnership, called it Jelonair, and set about sourcing and selling their new product, which rapidly became a range of products. Although it was slow at the beginning, things suddenly took off and for five years the business thrived. Howard and Josh moved from their home to nice premises, rapidly recruiting a staff of ten. Josh would have gone for cheaper premises and slower recruitment, but Howard told him that he needed to think big and not hold the business back.

Josh also felt uncomfortable with the partnership structure as the business grew, most particularly because Howard spent money very readily and took little interest in the financial side of the business. Josh persuaded him to agree to limited company status, partly to reduce their personal financial exposure, but also because it would be necessary in any case as they planned to raise money for investment. Howard had a pet project, which Josh was a little nervous about, which involved funding the development of a specialized cleaning product complete with its own dispenser. Josh knew that there could not be a better time to sell cleaning products to hospitals but was still uncomfortable about the financial exposure. However, he also recognized that one of the reasons why he was in business with Howard was because he knew that he tended to be overcautious, and Howard was a risk taker. Josh did not want to be accused of holding the business back.

Howard and Josh raised the funding and the development began. It took longer than expected and Howard became bored with the project. It was at this point that Josh noticed that a large sum had gone from the company account and been paid back three days later. Only he and Howard could sign company cheques, so he knew Howard must have taken the money. Although he was concerned that Howard had not mentioned it to him, he let it pass, since it had been so promptly replaced. This happened again over the next few months, generally small sums would go, and then be repaid. He asked Howard, who simply said that he had a few personal cash flow problems which he was in the process of sorting out, and not to worry, it was all under control. Since this was such uncharacteristic behaviour, Josh believed him and let the matter drop.

It was at this point that Howard's mother, Mary, rang Josh. Josh had met her a few times, and knew her to be a strong and direct woman, widowed many years before, and very fond of her only son. Mary said: 'Josh, I'm concerned at the amount of investment funds the company needs. Howard keeps telling me that I'll have to be patient, and I keep paying out, but now I've no more money that is free to invest, and Howard is asking for more. I thought you could give me your view of the situation.'

This left Josh with a dilemma. Mary had indeed invested £10,000 some time ago, but he was not aware of any other funding from her. If he asked, she would smell a rat. He decided that he needed to be loyal to Howard, for now, at least.

'I know it's frustrating, Mrs Ashby, but our new project is taking up more time and money than we planned. It will be a great product when it's ready, believe me. We can manage with the investment we have to date – Howard is just covering himself by asking for more. I don't think you should release tied investments now. I'm sure we'll start showing you a return soon.'

Josh went to Howard and told him about the call:

'Your mother says she has been investing regularly in the company, Howard, but there was only that initial £10,000, wasn't there?'

'Why was she ringing you, Josh?'

'I've no idea, Howard. She said you kept fobbing her off, so she wanted my view.'

'Take no notice, Josh, she's getting a bit forgetful now. I borrowed a little from her for personal stuff – she's probably got confused. You said the right thing, anyway. I'll go and see her tonight, and calm her down a bit – she's 80 next month, you know.' Josh did not think that Mary sounded confused at all, but there was nothing more he could do. As he left, he noticed that Howard had been viewing a betting website on his PC – it was not the first time that he had noticed this, and it did nothing to allay his fears.

Howard had a great network in the industry and he heard about a small company, selling cleaning utensils, which was in some financial difficulty. Howard and Josh investigated thoroughly, and liked Annette, the owner. Her problem was simple cash flow, and only small sums were involved. They arranged to buy a majority shareholding and keep her running the business. She readily agreed, and from then on she worked hard to build up sales, in which she was very successful.

One day she reported to Josh that a major sum had disappeared from her business account. It was obvious that Howard was responsible, and they confronted him. He blithely explained that this was money needed for reinvestment elsewhere, and refused to go into details. At this point, Josh decided to have a heart to heart with Howard. He knew that Howard's wife had left him just before they set up the business together, and that Howard had been playing the field for some time. He asked Howard to talk about the financial pressures that he was under, and mentioned the online betting, but Howard's response was glib: 'The online betting is peanuts, Josh, just an occasional distraction. The real problem was Lisa. I took her to Monaco for the weekend and she has expensive tastes, especially when it comes to the roulette wheel. I shan't be seeing her again though, she lost interest when she discovered I didn't have bottomless pockets, so not to worry.'

But Josh did worry. He had also observed Howard closing deals which he did not like the look of at all. He felt that Howard was behaving like someone who was desperate for money, perhaps someone who had caught the gambling bug. He went to see his old friend Jeremy, who knew all there was to know about business problems, and he told him the story. 'I think I may have to walk away from all this, Jeremy. Howard just isn't the man I set up in business with. He's draining the company dry. I can't trust him anymore, nor can I be associated with the kind of deals he's now doing.'

Jeremy went through the business numbers with Josh, and agreed that the situation was grave, but salvageable. Howard was the majority shareholder by 2 per cent. If that majority could be eroded, he could be voted out. This proved easier than expected because they were always trying to raise money, and so Josh went to Howard with a new investor, someone Jeremy knew. Since Howard was always keen to bring in more cash, he happily signed the share certificates that diluted his holding. If Howard had done the calculation, he could have worked out the effect, but he was too keen to get his hands on the money. An extraordinary general meeting was then called, and Howard was voted out. He reacted very badly, refused to leave, and accused Josh of conspiring against him. Eventually he stormed out, and Josh has not spoken to Howard since.

Jeremy then helped Josh to sort out the company finances since it was practically insolvent. The only major saleable asset was the new product. If they could sell it outright, then they would have enough money to pay all the creditors. Howard's share in the business could be given to him in the form of the cleaning products company, of which he would have sole ownership. This would leave Josh and Annette in a solid financial position to run the utensils company together.

Josh went to see all the creditors, and explained the situation. They could either wait and get their money back, or foreclose and get little or nothing. With Jeremy acting as intermediary, Howard agreed to take over the original business, and relinquish any interests in the rest. Josh already knew someone who was very interested in their new product, and with Jeremy's help he made a good deal, and paid off the creditors in full, with some funding left to invest in the utensils business.

At this point, Josh got a call from Mary, demanding to know what was going on. Her son would tell her nothing, it seemed, except that there would not be any new product from which to recover her investment.

'That's £55,000 I've invested in your operation – now tell me what you've done with it!'

'Mrs Ashby, I'm devastated to hear that, because this company has only seen £10,000 of your money, as far as I'm aware. Let me investigate and come back to you.'

Josh was convinced that no other funds had ever made their way into the company, and he discussed the issue with Jeremy. In the end, they decided that an independent audit was the only way to convince Mary of the facts.

Josh rang and told her this, and asked if she wanted to choose an auditor. She did, the audit was completed and indeed, there was only £10,000 of her money in the business. Josh went to see her with the report, and explained it to her. As he left, he said, 'I'm very sorry Mrs Ashby, but Howard seems to have some major debts, which is why we are no longer in business together. You still have shares in Howard's business, so I hope you can help him to make a success of it.' They exchanged glances and both knew how unlikely this was.

With the slate now clean, Josh put all his energy into the utensils business, which is growing steadily. He and Annette still work from home, and now they have taken on a full-time administrator, but will not move into office premises until their size justifies it. Josh looks back on Jelonair as a very harrowing experience, but feels he has learned a great deal from it and is operating more effectively as a result.

Lessons learned

Josh was keen to tell Helen, the company doctor, where things went wrong.

'Howard and I relied far too much on the fact that we had known each other well for ten years. That meant that we didn't set up the formal processes that a business needs. The most obvious of these was to have dual signatures on cheques. If we'd had that in place, I would have been in control, and would have seen the problem immediately. I did still see it pretty promptly, but Howard would have been forced to justify payments to me, and that would have brought the whole thing to a head much more quickly.

'When a business is set up, it's vital to get all the checks and balances in place, and not take them personally – just consider them as professional. Once the business is going, it's really hard to change, and then it does become personal.

'Obviously, the other mistake I made was in misjudging my partner. I do think that I can be excused to some degree for my slow reaction, because I believe that he did undergo a personality change during the time I knew him. Two things seem to have made the difference – his wife left him, and he became addicted to gambling. However, the change was gradual, and therefore more difficult to spot. He had a 15-year track record with me of being reliable and trustworthy – we had five good years of partnership working without any sign of a problem, and we'd worked together for ten years before that. I don't think you can blame me for giving him the benefit of the doubt in those circumstances. However, the big lesson I have learned is not that you can misjudge people, that's easily done, but that people you know can change and behave in ways you've never seen before, so you can't rely on them staying the same.

'Because of my reluctance to believe that Howard had changed, I was too slow in taking advice. I should have spoken to Jeremy earlier, in confidence, and got someone else's perspective on the situation. I tried to talk to my wife about it, but she isn't very interested in the business and has always liked Howard, so she reinforced my view that I should do nothing and hope that things would sort themselves out.

'When I did take advice I really did take it. Jeremy has been brilliant in all respects and I don't know what I'd have done without him. Well, I do, actually. I would have just walked away and lost everything, so I've resolved in future that whenever I face some uncertainty, I shall always take advice.

'Part of the reason why the business was in such bad shape was because of our new product. This project had taken far longer than we estimated, which all projects do, but there was also the fact that Howard had taken his eye off the ball and got bored. Again, I should have done something about that sooner, and had less faith in Howard – I just left him to it because it was his baby. Looked at financially, it was very much my baby too. It has come right in the end, because we had an asset to sell and could pay off all our debts but, when I think about it, the product could have transformed our business, and that is such a pity.

'Having said that, Howard has taught me how to take a risk on developing a new product and, when the time is right, I may try it myself. However, I'm not nearly so clear about the over-investment in people and premises. I know I'm overcautious, and it would not have been an over-investment if Howard hadn't gone off the rails and the project and his other deals had come good. In the end, it must be down to how much faith you have in your future success, and how fast you plan to grow.'

Success tactics

Here is a summary of Helen's conclusions, which fall under the following headings:

- Management controls
- Ability to take calculated risks
- Plan and evaluate
- Getting and taking advice
- Flexibility in business structure.

Management controls

'I have seen many partnerships fail, this is quite common, but it does seem that Josh was dealing with two different people in the business: a stable, trustworthy Howard, and then the financial liability that he became. Josh's willingness to continue trusting him is therefore very understandable, but the reality is that in the hard world of business, you do not argue with the facts. People change for many reasons, and in business, severe financial pressure often results in very undesirable behaviour, which appears completely out of character.

'As Josh points out, the business should have been set up with all the formal controls in place. This is one of the key elements of good business management that was missing from Jelonair.'

Ability to take calculated risks

'Josh and Howard epitomize the two extremes in business: think big and spend with a vision of huge success, versus grow steadily and build only on firm foundations. If Josh had not been over-compensating for his cautious nature, instead of allowing Howard to have his head completely, he would have forced Howard to do more financial planning, and they might have chosen a middle path.

'Having said that, many big successes in business involve a huge leap of faith and major risk. The owners build successful businesses because they also have conviction in the outcome and a drive to achieve. If you have these feelings, then you may wish to make the leap. What is absolutely certain is that you should not take the risk if you do not have the drive and conviction to go with it.'

Plan and evaluate

'Jelonair was technically insolvent in the end because of Howard's mismanagement of the project, his misappropriation of funds, together with the combination of unprofitable sales and high running costs. Josh needed to take a firm line here, with tight financial planning and review. If this achieved nothing with Howard, it would almost certainly have provoked Josh into seeking advice much earlier.

'Managing your partner is just as important as managing your staff. Obviously there was the financial element, but there was also the fact that Howard was bored with the development project. This almost certainly contributed to delays and Josh could have been more proactive here and, after reviews with Howard, could have volunteered to "help" or looked for some way of rekindling Howard's enthusiasm. This might not have delivered a great deal, but it would have brought Josh closer to the project and its financial ramifications.'

Getting and taking advice

'Josh has learned this lesson well – he needed advice early on. It was understandable that he didn't have a business buddy since that was Howard's role, but he did know Jeremy already, he didn't have to go looking for him, and it would have been so easy, as he says, to talk to him in confidence. A sense of disloyalty obviously stood in his way, but he needed to be loyal to the business, for both his and Howard's sakes, and someone else could have helped him to see this.'

Flexibility in the business structure

'It was fortunate, in the end, that Howard created an asset for the business to sell. It is hard to deal with a partner who is out of financial control but Josh should, in any case, have taken a firmer line on cost control. Their offices were a bigger liability than they actually needed, and decisions to hire more staff were taken too lightly, so they had more financial exposure as a result. Without this, Josh would now have more in his pocket to invest in his utensils company.'

Your health check

Key questions to ask:

1 Are there any personal issues I need to address with my colleagues?
2 Do I have formal business controls in place?
3 How comfortable am I with my current cost structure?
4 Have I got the balance right between risk and caution?
5 Do I have a written plan for any new ventures I am undertaking?
6 Do I need advice on any aspect of the business, especially if it is worrying me?

02

running out of cash

Running out of cash is the most common reason why small businesses fail. This problem can have a number of causes: lack of financial understanding, and/or lack of management control are the most frequent internal issues; bad debts and market and economic problems are the usual external culprits.

This case study is a clear illustration of how cash flow problems can strike the unsuspecting, and yet leave the company stronger in the end.

Company profile: Abacus E-media

Abacus E-media is a company which has majored in Web-based design, development and hosting since 1995, but Steve Feigen was a co-founder long before that, in 1977, when the Web did not exist. The company began in those early days as a specialist software supplier and, as the IT market developed, it moved into hardware, selling microcomputers. Then the hardware market became more competitive, and in 1986 came the crunch decision to move out of hardware and concentrate on software, to provide content management for clients in online publishing.

Abacus has therefore undergone several major changes in its life and, since it also operates in the very volatile IT marketplace, it is not surprising that it has hit a number of cash flow problems in its time. These happened either as a result of making changes in the business to meet the changing needs of the market or because of market collapses, typified by the bursting of the dot.com bubble at the end of the twentieth century.

Steve remembers two occasions in particular where cash flow was a problem:

'Over the years I have hit a number of cash flow problems, but two stand out, one in the 1990s, when my house was on the line, and we had to manage cash daily; and the other one was when the IT market stalled at the end of the dot.com boom. Hundreds of Web agencies closed at that time but we survived, partly because we were supplying established businesses and not just the new dot.coms. Our revenue reduced by half and the profits were tiny, but we never did make a loss. I had 32 staff and had to lay off 8, leaving me with a very strong team of 24, but this still left too much cost, so we gave staff a choice: either more cuts, or everyone would go on to a 4-day week, including me. They were a very tight team, so it didn't take them long to decide to take the 4-day option, and that arrangement continued for 18 months.

'Apart from cutting costs dramatically, we immediately threw all our sales effort into the public sector, which was the only place money was being spent at that time. Although we had few public sector clients to start with, we grew and kept a very solid portfolio in that area, which made a huge difference during those IT recession years. Now we have the best of both worlds as our publishers have come back and we have a good growth record.'

'Really, by the time this crisis hit, although the market was tough, it was not nearly as bad for us in cash flow terms as in 1991, because we'd learned so much from our earlier experiences, and because we're much stronger financially.'

Lessons learned

Steve explained to Helen, the company doctor, how much he had learned from the cash flow crises he had suffered.

'We became much better at forecasting and cash flow, and understanding the need for reserves. However, looking back, I think it was the techniques that we developed, having faced this problem a few times, that kept us out of trouble, and they are not about the obvious things, cash and sales, but more about how you operate in a crisis.

'I am not a reflective kind of person, I tend to see a problem and then take action. I don't sit around thinking about it. I'm also a fighter and an optimist, which means that I think positively, and don't really think about failure unless it happens. For example, whenever I've been in this situation, it has never occurred to me that bankruptcy was an option. I always believed that we would find a way through, and I think that this belief was a key reason that we survived. Just applying the techniques would probably not have been enough.

'The first technique is about preserving a positive mental state, which is quite hard to do when people are phoning you up all the time, demanding money. Dealing with these calls drags you down. It becomes difficult to stay positive when you are getting threats every day, so the first priority is to shield yourself from these calls.

'I had an excellent accountant who worked for me, and she would handle all the calls and only tell me about them at our cash flow forecasting meetings. These meetings varied in frequency, depending on the crisis point, from daily to monthly. Whenever a meeting took place, she would tell me all about who called for what. We would look at the forecast, decide a plan of action, and then there would be no more discussion until the next meeting, and I would return to my positive state, knowing that we had done all we could do at that point. Normally in this situation, my key action would be to win more sales, so being positive was part of the solution, not about pretending there wasn't a problem.

'As far as handling suppliers goes, I've always found it best to go and see them if you have a real problem. I would always acknowledge that they are due full payment, and would never pretend that I was querying the invoice, or the cheque was 'lost' in the post. These crises have always happened to me at times when the market or the economy was a major problem, so I have always been able to argue that my problem was caused externally, not by my company's incompetence. At times like these, clients might delay or default on a payment to us, which made things even worse.

'I would therefore explain all this, perhaps stress that a client of mine had defaulted, to win as much sympathy as possible. I would also tell suppliers about my action plan to fix the problem, and with that I would propose a programme of staged or delayed payments. The delay period might be quite long before the first payment because I would want to be as sure as I could be that I could keep my promises. Once a payment plan was agreed, I would stick to it, come what may, and I've never defaulted on one of these arrangements because you lose all credibility if you do. They won't believe you a second time. I've even done this with the VAT man and the Inland Revenue and, as long as you have a good reason to delay payment, have a credible plan to make it, and then keep your promises, this strategy works.

'The next technique is to ensure that clients pay you on time. To do this, which is good business practice anyway, my accountant would ring up the person who was responsible for physically paying the bill about a week beforehand, to make sure that everything was approved and to find out when the cheque run would be. If there were any glitches with signatures, etc., that gave her time to sort them out and, with her gentle and friendly reminder, they would not miss her cheque off the run, or do any of the other things that mean that payments are delayed, whether deliberately or accidentally. On some occasions, she might even manage to get payment early.

'Another of my strategies is never to go to the bank when you're desperate. Effectively, we used our suppliers to get the additional credit we needed when we were in trouble. I have always worked at my relationship with the bank: I was never aggressive or complaining, and I didn't create any waves – moaning about their charges, for example. They always saw me at my most positive: when we needed money for expansion. I've been very successful in obtaining money from them – we had a 9:1 gearing* at one time, but I would never go near them when times are bad. I've always understood that bank managers get a black mark against them when a business goes bust, so I've never wanted to be even close to that in their eyes, and we've rarely exceeded our overdraft limit. Of course they ask a few questions at our annual meetings, but I've been well prepared for those.

'People often blame their problems on banks – it's easy to do, but some of that is down to the way you manage them.

'Your home life also needs careful managing at times like these. I have the ability to switch off completely when I want to, which unfortunately my wife does not share. When we were in danger of losing our house, I felt that I had to tell her, and she made herself ill with worry as a result. It was hard to decide whether or not to keep it from her, but she did have a right to know.

'When I leave the office, I know I've done all I can do for the day, and there is no point in worrying any more, and so I don't! I get on the train, bury myself in a good paperback, and don't think about work anymore until I get to the office door the next morning. Once my wife knew about the problem, she would want to discuss everything in the evening, whereas I had switched off, so it didn't really help either of us that she knew. I'm practical, not emotional. I see a business as a living organism, and you have to do whatever is necessary to keep it alive. I was in control, and comfortable that I was doing all I could to save the company. She was not involved in the business so she was, in effect, a spectator, and she chose, very understandably, to put all her energies into worrying, which made her ill. All completely unnecessary, since things worked out fine, but it's difficult to explain that to someone who thinks they might be homeless at any moment.

'If I faced these problems again, I'd know exactly what to do, except I still wouldn't be sure whether to tell my wife!'

*Their finance was 90 per cent borrowing and 10 per cent of their own money.

Success tactics

Helen's comments fall under the following headings:

- A clear focus
- Plan and evaluate
- A financial feel for the business
- Good business relationships
- Getting the best from your people
- Ability to balance home and work
- A feel for the market
- Commitment to business success.

Helen says, 'Hearing all that Steve has said, he has not only described the lessons he has learned, but has also formulated a plan for future success which is very impressive. As well as commenting on his success tactics, I would also like to highlight some of the things that are implicit in what he says.'

A clear focus

'Steve's ability to focus is remarkable, not least for the wonderful capability he has to switch off that focus, or direct it elsewhere at will. How wonderful it would be for life's worriers to tell themselves not to, and just stop! This is not a skill which is easily acquired, otherwise Steve would surely have taught it to his wife. The lesson we can all take away here is that Steve was absolutely focused on spending his working time in the very best way possible. At the end of the day, he knew he had done his best, and so he switched off until the next morning. We might not all manage the off switch quite so successfully, but it is easier when you know that you have put all you can into the day, and have not just worked hard, but worked hard at the right things.'

Plan and evaluate

'Steve knew he was doing the right things because he had made a full evaluation of his situation, and had a very clear plan to resolve it. He had a plan for cutting costs, a plan for selling to a brand new market, and a plan for managing cash.'

A financial feel for the business

'Steve chose his accountant well, and the discipline of daily cash flow forecasts in a crisis teaches you very quickly about the realities of business. The real lesson here is not to wait for a crisis before you apply that discipline. You won't need to do it daily, but a monthly review will be instructive. You can then change this it to quarterly if things are very comfortable, or make it weekly if they are not.

'Steve raises the subject of reserves, which are obviously a useful cash cushion to call upon, and in theory every company should have reserves. However, this is hard to do when you are expanding and ploughing all you earn back into the business. Getting to a position where you have a reasonable level of reserves – say at least enough to pay one or two months' outgoings – is something to aim for. Obviously, the funds need to be very accessible, but balance this with making the money deliver a good return.'

Good business relationships

'This is exemplified by the way Steve managed his creditors, with face-to-face meetings, and never failed on his payment plan. I cannot entirely support his view of how to handle the bank. He is right that it is better to go to them in good times rather than bad, and certainly I agree that you should never go to them in a crisis but always try to anticipate and go to them before disaster hits. They want to see that you are alert to problems, and you want to appear as in control as possible. Having said that, there are times when extending your overdraft or taking out a loan are the only solutions to major cash problems. It is a tribute to Steve's cash management that he never had to take that step.'

Getting the best from your people

'The teamwork between Steve and his accountant is outstanding, and Steve did tell me that it was an emotional moment when he thanked her publicly at their celebration event some time afterwards. It was also an original and effective way to cut costs by moving to a four-day week and by offering staff the choice of this or more redundancies. Steve's inclusion of himself in this demonstrates his commitment to his team and kept them motivated during difficult times, and it built flexibility into his cost structure.'

Ability to balance home and work

'Steve's ability to switch off and not worry serves him very well here, and means that he could get a real break from work at home, were it not for the fact that he had told his wife about the problems and she made herself ill with worry. Commenting from a purely business perspective, it would have been better for Steve not to say anything, particularly as everything turned out well in the end. However, this has to be a personal decision.'

A feel for the market

'Steve makes little of this, but his decision to move all his efforts from the private to the public sector was a major shift, and one that was made very quickly indeed. Steve would tell you that it was a simple decision: his market had collapsed, and the only place that had a sure supply of money was the public sector. Recognizing this quickly and then adapting to a new market shows a high level of market awareness and unusual business agility.'

Commitment to business success

'My final comment is that Steve showed an unwavering commitment to his company's success throughout. The clear belief that he could win carried him through when so many fell by the wayside. He illustrates perfectly Henry Ford's famous words: 'Whether you believe that you can do a thing or not, you are right.'

Your health check

Key questions to ask:

1 Do I have a clear written plan for achieving my business aims?
2 Is what I do each day my very best contribution to achieving those aims?
3 Do I have a feel for the way my business works financially?
4 How often do I monitor cash flow?
5 Do I have reserves or plan to have some?
6 Do I work at my business relationships with suppliers of all kinds, from my bank to my computer expert?

03

lack of management controls

Many things look easy when done by an expert and, indeed, whole processes can become invisible to those who have never had cope with them, such as running a conference, for example. To the outsider, it just happens; to the conference organizer, it is a huge task. The same can be said of running a business. People can take the simple view that you just deliver the product or service, get paid and put the money in the bank. They might see finding new customers as a challenge, but if you have enough to be going on with, then you can just keep delivering, and that's all there is to it! This case study shows how quickly a well-managed business can change, and how easy it is to take management controls for granted.

Company profile: Crowell & Son

Crowell & Son was a printing company set up at the beginning of the twentieth century in Derby, England, by John Crowell, who gradually built an excellent reputation in the area. He handed a flourishing business to his son, Ben, who ran it successfully for two years before he was killed in a car accident, leaving his wife Betty and son John, aged ten, to inherit the business.

Betty immediately had approaches from others wanting to buy the business, but she had other ideas. She was a strong and ambitious woman, bored by being a housewife at home. She had always taken a close interest in the business, and now it was all hers. She was tough, astute and hard working. Under her management, the business flourished as never before, and she sent her only child to the very best schools to prepare him for his future role as the head of Crowell.

John did not view this prospect with enthusiasm. He was very artistic and wanted to go to art college. His mother insisted on business studies. In the end, he managed to find a compromise course on design in business, which he convinced his mother would enable him to bring a new skill to Crowell and, seeing the business potential, Betty agreed.

When John joined the business, he was obliged to do every job, including running the brand new five-colour press bought for cash for a six-figure sum. This was a huge investment for the company, and used most of its reserves. There were two older presses that were no longer needed, but they would wait to sell at the right time, Betty had decided.

When he had worked his way round the business, Betty began the process of training John in all aspects of her role. He was not very interested and could not see the point of much of what his mother did. She seemed to check and double-check everything. Betty was obsessive about cash and collecting debts, and would go to see people personally if they did not pay up on time. He knew the business had reserves of cash, so waiting a few more days hardly seemed to matter, but he passed no comment.

John soon began to do speculative design work and showed it to his mother. 'Not the right time for that,' was her reply, as they could hardly cope with the print business coming through the door. Over the next three years, John would try again from time to time, but always got the same answer. He was bored and he was beginning to think that he would have to go and set up on his own, when his mother had a massive heart attack and died a week later.

It took John only a short while to realize how much he had relied on his mother. He regretted not having taken her training sessions seriously. He immediately thought of starting design work, but he had his hands full with the printing business so he decided to recruit someone to run it as soon as possible. He struggled with all the numbers and called in Eric, their accountant, to help him out. He explained that he wanted to get a manager to run the business for him. Eric pointed to a decline in the sales figures, and suggested that a salesperson would be a better investment, together with a junior accounts clerk to deal with the basic administration. That way some of the burden would be taken from John.

John saw that this was sensible, and he placed two advertisements in the local paper. He had a string of applicants for the accounts job, and chose Emma, the prettiest one. He did not bother with references – he had already decided.

After two weeks, there were no applicants for the sales job, but then Larry rang and came to see John. He was older than John expected, but seemed very assured and experienced, so after a 40-minute chat, John took him on.

John hoped to start his design work as soon as the two new recruits were on board, but of course it took time to train Emma, and Larry was on a month's notice and then had some holiday. There were also problems with the printing staff, and a customer was asking for some work to be redone. John did not remember his mother having to deal with issues like this, but then, he had taken little notice of what she did.

John decided that Crowell would benefit from a new image, and set about redesigning the logo and letterhead. He thought that if he kept his head down, all the problems would eventually sort themselves out. Three months later, Eric came to tell him that Emma was incompetent, but John insisted that she was just learning the ropes and needed more time. That also explained why Larry had not sold anything, either.

Six months later, Eric convinced him that Emma had to go, and pointed to a serious decline in sales. Larry had still to produce an order, but he had 'a great pipeline'. John decided to give him three more months. In the meantime, his best printer had left – he was not sure why – and there were still problems in the print room, and increasing requests for work to be redone, as well as many invoice queries.

Two months later, Eric came to see John, and told him he was about to run out of cash. John did not believe him, 'We've always had plenty of cash, loads of reserves. We can't have run out!'

Eric reminded him that the new press had consumed most of those reserves, and they had still not sold off the old machines. He pointed out that the print market was in serious decline, and mentioned three companies that had gone bust in the past six months. 'You are just relying on repeat orders from existing customers – you are making no new sales at all. You've got to do something now, John, otherwise you won't have a business.'

They sat down and worked out an action plan:

1 Collect debts now to cover cash flow.
2 Consider factoring debt.
3 Sell old machines.
4 Fire Larry.
5 Cut costs.
6 Work out sales plan for print.
7 Diversify into added value services.

John tried debt collecting for the first time and did not like it, nor did he get any money immediately. Suddenly, the seriousness of the situation hit him. He was in danger of losing everything. He felt sick at the thought. This feeling stayed with him for some months. He woke up feeling sick with worry, and he went to bed in the same state. He was forced to go to the bank, who generously offered to help him out with a mortgage on his house. This bought him some time, though no comfort.

With Eric's help, John explored factoring options, and chose a company to factor all his invoices: now he gets at least 80 per cent of all payments within 24 hours. It costs him a small percentage, of course, but he knows it is worth it. He sold the old machines, but as the market was so clearly in decline, they went for half the value shown in the books after depreciation, thereby creating a large paper loss.

John fired Larry, who had still not produced a single order. He paid him off correctly, and was shocked to receive an unfair dismissal claim from Larry's solicitor a month later. It proved groundless, but it took John time and money to confirm that, using a specialist employment lawyer. John then paid for the correct wording of the response, and nothing more was heard from Larry.

John went through the operating costs, but there was little to trim without cutting down the firm's work capacity. His mother had run things very tightly.

John was at a loss when it came to sales. Tim, who ran the printing side was actually quite good with clients, but he could hardly send him out on the road. Eric suggested telesales. His neighbour, Anita, had a young family and wanted a part-time job. She had a telesales background and might be interested. She was! She now works four mornings a week, either selling directly, or making appointments for Tim. She produced her first order, small though it was, in her second week, and has gone from strength to strength. She had a friend, Ros, in similar circumstances, and John took her on to do the afternoon shift.

The final part of John's plan was to diversify, and finally he was able to start on the design work he had wanted to do for years. He decided that he would bridge the gap between online media and paper media, and promoted his designs as being suitable for both. Having given this brief to Anita and Ros, he found he soon had far more work than he could deal with, and was being asked to design websites as well as brochures. From then on, the business has not looked back, and the balance has shifted from a print company to a design company that also does printing. After the period of pain, sales have resumed the upward trend line set by John's mother, Betty, and John is beginning to enjoy the business.

John has also acquired some of Betty's habits. He does not have to worry about debt collection, but he does keep a daily cash flow record. A simple sheet for each month, which he fills in manually. It has a line for each day of the month, and then three columns: In, Out and Balance. He keeps meaning to computerize it, but does not quite get round to it because it forces him to check daily on orders and bills to be paid. He learned the discipline the hard way – when he put his house on the line – and although he hardly uses his overdraft now and is accelerating the repayment of his mortgage, he still finds it useful to keep his finger on the pulse of the business.

Lessons learned

John knows that he made many mistakes, but also feels that his mother, Betty, made at least one which was to take her market for granted. She stopped John diversifying early on, which would have transformed the business as the print market declined. Although Betty died when business was still very good, there were warning signs that she ignored. The move to online media had already begun to happen, and if Betty had been watching trends closely, she would have responded by building tomorrow's business, instead of putting all her energies into today's. Betty should also have sold the old machines at once, and not waited, because it was obvious, when you took the trouble to look, that prices would only go one way.

In talking to Helen, the company doctor, John acknowledges that he threw away the opportunity to learn from his mother, and many of the things he now does, he has learned to do the hard way.

'I was still the spoiled child, not getting my own way. All that figure work was boring, so why should I bother, when my mother did it all so well? I should have thought ahead, of course I should, but she was very strong and healthy, and only 56, so you can't really blame me for not thinking about what would happen when she retired. After she died, I realized just how little I knew, and my response was to take refuge in something I did know – company image design. That was the last thing we needed at that time, but it gave me something apparently useful to do so that I did not have to face up to all the difficult things that needed doing.

'It's obvious now that I let the company go to pot. I made stupid recruitment decisions, I ignored staff problems, and I didn't want to look at the numbers. I was so lucky to have Eric. He forced me to face up to things, and even then we had to run out of cash before I really owned the problem.

'It's so frustrating to think that I had the solution in my hands all the time. If only I'd started my design work earlier, but then without the right people selling, it might not have taken off in the way it did, and the online/on paper proposition might not have been so strong in the early days.

'I've worked out what I'm good at and bad at, so I never make recruitment decisions alone, ever, and I always take Eric's advice on any financial decision. I'm getting better at managing people now I've grown up a bit, and I'm not bad at selling, provided there's a design element. I look at cash flow daily, and I keep my ear to the ground all the time for market trends. For me, the biggest lessons out of all this are to watch cash and your marketplace like a hawk.'

Success tactics

Helen, the company doctor, observed that John certainly had learned a great deal from his experience. Here are her comments in the following areas:

- Management controls/To lead or to manage the business
- A financial feel for the business
- A feel for the market / Plan and evaluate
- Getting and taking advice
- Getting the best from your people
- A passion for what you do.

Management controls/To lead or to manage the business

'John did provide leadership in taking the company in a new direction, but otherwise he had no grasp of management at all and tried to abdicate responsibility for it. Betty ran a tight ship, which John entirely took for granted. Here is a list of some of the things she did, many of which remained invisible to John:

1 Managing staff to get high quality and good productivity.
2 Monitoring the price/quality balance of staff output.
3 Managing finance to keep the business profitable and cash positive.
4 Managing debtors personally.
5 Keeping suppliers on their toes both for price and delivery.
6 Maintaining personal relationships with key clients.

'It is not surprising that the print team went off the rails after Betty died. John had no idea that she managed it at all, never mind how she managed it. This is so often the case with good management: it becomes invisible when done well, and only becomes evident when things go wrong. Although John has improved in this area, he would benefit from some training or coaching to help him move from adequate to excellent.'

A financial feel for the business

'The fact that John still completes a daily cash flow forecast underlines how financially aware he has become. This is a useful discipline for many small companies to acquire. They could do it on a weekly or monthly basis, depending on their exposure, but doing it themselves keeps their finger on the pulse of the business. No pulse means no business – it's as simple and as catastrophic as that. Factoring debt can be a very good way of guaranteeing your cash flow. Make the decision based on the deal you can get and your own company's debt collection skills and inclinations.'

A feel for the market/Plan and evaluate

'John is right that he and his mother should have sat down a long time ago to review their market and the way it was going. They could then have examined options, studied the competition, and come up with a new market plan. This would have taken time, but would have been the perfect project for John. He would have seen that lots of printers were diversifying into design and that he needed a differentiator to build for the future.'

Getting and taking advice

'It's not every accountant who is as proactive and street-wise as Eric. He was an excellent adviser to John, but it is really important not to rely on your accountant for business advice. He or she might be the right person, but it is very likely that your accountant will not offer advice unless you ask for it. This means that there is a serious danger that you interpret silence as approval. Do not fall into this trap. Just because they produce your numbers does not mean that the numbers are healthy. If in doubt, ask.

'The company needed a market adviser early on, too, but John's mother was in the classic 'If it isn't broken, don't fix it' mould where the market was concerned. It is hard to seek advice to change when your present plan seems to be working perfectly well, but that's the secret of real success.

'John desperately needed a business buddy, and Eric was not close enough to him to give the sharp, wake-up call he really needed early on. When you have a relationship with someone where no fees are involved, you can afford to be honest and say what you think. John needed a friendly buddy to tell him that he was behaving like an ostrich, making silly recruitment decisions, and losing valuable staff.'

Getting the best from your people

'With John's attitude and inexperience, it is hardly surprising that Emma and Larry did not deliver. Larry might have fooled a far more experienced person than John, however, as salespeople can be very difficult to recruit. It often happens that if someone falls into the 'salesman' category, as they are often caricatured, with the right 'chat' and the foot in the door approach, then they are not good salespeople. Taking a fresh approach with people like Tim and Anita can often pay dividends. Obviously, you need to choose carefully, but both Tim and Anita had demonstrated abilities to build good relationships with clients, and Crowell now has a much more cost-effective sales solution.'

A passion for what you do

'John's mother consistently refused to allow her son to follow his passion, which distorted his response to the business. As soon as he was free to do what he liked, he did just that, and ignored the rest. Thanks to Eric, he still has a business, and he is at last able to enjoy it.

'We don't all have mothers interfering in business life, but many other things can stop us from doing what we love, and the consequences can be just as severe.'

Your health check

Key questions to ask:

1 Do I take refuge in my comfort zone, instead of addressing business issues?
2 Have I structured the business so that I can do what I love?
3 Do I have a really good sales resource?
4 Do I see and feel how my cash flows?
5 How well is my business managed in the three areas of:
   a Administration
   b Execution
   c Staff?

04 funding problems

The process of obtaining funding and managing your investors can be a huge challenge for a small business. Often companies are looking for money only and do not realize until it is too late that when the money arrives, the investor comes with it! The roller-coaster story of Axilia Surveys shows just how easy it is to choose the wrong investor, and the disastrous consequences that may follow.

Company profile: Axilia Surveys

Vincent Delaney had worked for some years in the Human Resources (HR) department of a large multinational company, and then he moved into HR consultancy. He specialized in employee surveys, but became frustrated when he wanted to do specific marketing in his area and found that there were never any funds available. Vincent felt that he was the poor relation because the focus of the company was on rewards and compensation, and there was little interest in staff attitude surveys.

Vincent had never liked corporate life anyway, and so he decided to set up on his own. He had cultivated a good network of contacts, and he looked for an investor. He talked to a market research company, the XRZ Group, that specialized in focus groups. XRZ saw the synergy between his business and theirs, and agreed to put in 75 per cent of the funding. Vincent provided the other 25 per cent, remortgaging his house to do so. XRZ provided office space, which suited Vincent very well, as they were based on the edge of Bristol, close to his home. Vincent called his new company Axilia Surveys.

All went well to begin with and, from a staff of two, the business grew to a staff of eight, with an annual turnover of £1.5 million. Vincent was pleased with progress, but was surprised to find that XRZ was consistently critical of his performance. He was told that he was spending too much money on hardware and software, and he realized that they did not really understand his business, which required more capital investment than theirs.

The spending issue rang alarm bells for Vincent and, after further discussions, it became apparent that the business was in serious trouble. Vincent said, 'They mistook assets shown in the balance sheet for cash! They made the classic mistake of believing that a profitable business meant a cash-rich business. As soon as I understood this I knew I had to get out, but I had to get out anyway, as they were about to run out of cash!'

Vincent looked for another investor and, after some intensive searching, found Hugan Investments, two HR consultants who had sold off their own business very profitably, and were now looking for investment opportunities. They bought Axilia for £1, thereby solving a problem for XRZ by taking Axilia off its hands.

Vincent breathed a huge sigh of relief at this point, 'The situation with XRZ had become very difficult to deal with. The directors were permanently at each other's throats, and Axilia was a convenient scapegoat of which they all took advantage. The managing director was drinking heavily, and showing signs of paranoia.' Vincent and his team had a permanent minder on the day of the sale to ensure that they did not run off with anything that did not belong to them, and they were escorted from the premises when the deal was done.

However, Vincent's relief did not last long. Hugan Investments, who Vincent believed to be his saviours, were not the cash-rich operation he thought they were. To his horror, he discovered that their business was funded by massive overdrafts, and high interest rates were eating any money they made. He realized that they had been looking to his company to change their fortunes, whereas he was looking to them for the same thing.

This was a very difficult time, and Hugan Investments were constantly breathing down Vincent's neck. He could see that the situation was looking dire for Hugan, but he could do little about it, other than try to make as much money as possible with Axilia, but this was never going to generate enough revenue fast enough to save Hugan Investments and, if they went down, they would almost certainly take Axilia with them:

'I was under huge pressure and, looking back now, I wonder how I coped. My wife was very supportive and, despite the fact that she was stuck at home with three small children and could do nothing practical to help, she always gave me the feeling that she had faith in my ability to pull through. That made a big difference. What also helped was the fact that I'd been going to the gym every day for the past 12 months, and was really fit. I think without these personal foundations I might have ended up a gibbering wreck!' Disaster was not long in coming: 'Hugan folded and, because of the nature of the cross guarantees that were made, I was in danger of losing everything, including my house. I really had jumped from the frying pan into the fire!' The inevitable followed. The bank foreclosed but, because Axilia was profitable, the bank sent in an administrator rather than the liquidator.

'The administrator asked me how I estimated costs for a survey. When I told him this was largely based on experience and not on a set formula, he told me that he was not prepared to take on the business with that level of risk. It hardly seemed much of a risk to me but, at the time, businesses were going bust all over the place, and these people didn't mess about. They were making lots of money, and could afford to walk away. They arrived in the morning and said they'd be back at 4 p.m. when they would close the company down unless I could find the money to buy it.

'Well, of course I didn't have any money – I was about to lose my house! I was desperate, so I just phoned people I knew, and did the selling job of my life. I phoned six people, asking for £50,000, on the spot. Unbelievably the sixth one said, 'Who do I make the cheque out to?'

'I had known this chap, Adrian, for some years, both as a colleague and as a client, but we were not close. I had given him some particularly good advice on one occasion – I told him his prices were too low, and that he should raise them by 10 per cent. He did and was very grateful. I think that was one of the reasons why he trusted me. He didn't ask to see the numbers, he just provided the funds and, of course, I gave him half the company in return, although he didn't ask for it. Gradually, over time, I have bought back most of his shares, so he has made a very handsome return, but few people would have taken that chance. I was very lucky to find him.

'Armed with funds, I was ready for the 4 p.m. meeting. I told the administrator that I would buy the company name and good will, but leave them with the debtors and creditors, and I would also help them to collect the debts. They asked me how much, and I took a deep breath and said '£8,000'. To my amazement they accepted the deal. I realize now that they had little choice. There was little to be gained by liquidating the company. There was little to sell if I was not part of it, so the best way out was to get me to buy it.'

Vincent negotiated a short-term lease with the landlords, who were only too keen to keep him as there was a shortage of tenants in the area. He also collected payment from his clients, blaming everything on the parent company, and reassuring them at the same time that it would be business as usual in future.

The main creditor was the Inland Revenue, but there were also four trade creditors, and Vincent was careful to explain all the problems to them and to ensure that they understood that future business would be done on very generous terms, to try to compensate for what they had lost. He has now rebuilt all of those relationships.

Today, 12 years later, Axilia has a turnover of about £5 million, and employs 40 staff. Vincent was determined that it would be third time lucky because he would build the business slowly and cautiously, with no borrowings of any kind. He recognizes that this has held back the company's growth, but this is not an issue for him:

'I had a huge desire to work for myself, and to be independent. I also had a desire to make some money, but I have no urge to make a bid for world domination of the survey market! I do not see growth as a worthwhile goal in itself. We continue to grow gently, largely to keep the staff happy and give them an ongoing challenge, but our growth is all self-funded. I won't ever get into debt again.'

Lessons learned

Talking to Alan, the company doctor, Vincent was emphatic about what he would do and not do again:

'I would check out my investors so carefully if I had my time again. It's easy to get yourself into the role of supplicant when you're looking for investment funding but, as you can see from my experience, this is a two-way relationship and you not only need to check on whether they have the money and where it's coming from, but also on what their expectations are of their involvement in the running of the company.

'My first investor didn't really understand my business but, more importantly, couldn't tell the difference between cash and profit. It's amazing that they survived as long as they did. My second investors didn't really have any money, just big bank loans, and they also failed to understand that Axilia could not generate money quickly. My third investor was a dream: he had real money; he did not want any say in the running of the business; he trusted my judgement; and he's been happy for me to buy back his shares. It really was third time lucky for me, and the only credit that I can claim is that I built a good business network, and I helped him out in the past with, at the time, no expectation of a return. How richly I have been repaid!

'One of the reasons why I didn't evaluate my first two investors was because I wasn't clear enough about the financial side of things. I knew all the theory, but I wasn't really comfortable with balance sheets and cash flow forecasts – I certainly am now! What I should have done was to bring in an accountant friend to help me – I just didn't think of it at the time. When people tell you they have the money to invest in your company, you're just so pleased to get it. It seems as if you're looking a gift horse in the mouth to ask to see their accounts.

'The other thing I've learned is that just running a successful business is not enough. Axilia has been successful throughout. We have grown steadily and always been profitable, but if your success is built on unstable foundations, then it counts for little. All success did for me was to put me in front of the administrator, rather than the liquidator, which almost amounted to the same thing.

'The bank that made the administration recommendation would not deal with me again after I bought the business from the administrator, despite the fact that they knew only too well that I was running a profitable business. I didn't press them, but I assume that once tarred with that brush, they don't want to touch you. The problem was that at the time I was with Hugan's bank – I'd had no chance to build a separate relationship with them. I'm on excellent terms with my current bank, especially as I am always in credit and have never borrowed a thing, but I know how different things could be. I make our relationship as positive as possible, in all senses, and if I needed them now, I'm as confident as one can be that they would help.

'I'm also much better equipped to deal with problems now. I should have taken advice, and not waited for Hugan Investments to fold. I didn't know a thing about administration, but I could see disaster coming, and I should have pre-empted it, or at least been prepared for the worst. When companies face the administrator, they are mostly like frightened rabbits in car headlights – they haven't a clue and they're in shock. In fact, the administrators are businesspeople like everyone else, and you can negotiate with them, like everyone else. They were making squillions at the time from all the businesses going bust, which meant that they had little time for me. I was a tiny, tiny fish of little or no value to them. I might have done an even better deal with them if I'd known the score. I wouldn't have found a better investor, but I might have done it in a more orderly fashion, not in the four hours I had to stave off liquidation. I can't think now why I didn't take any action when I saw how things were with Hugan Investments. I was just hoping for the best, and focusing all of my attention on running Axilia. It was head in the sand stuff, I now realize.

'What I did right was to have my personal life in good order. I was very fit, and had lots of support at home. I have always tried to keep a good balance in my life. It's hard when you're setting up a business, but it's been a goal I've always had as a priority, and so I've made it happen.'

Success tactics

After a thorough review of Axilia's current financial situation, here are Alan's comments, which fall under the following headings:

- Getting and taking advice
- A financial feel for the business
- Flexibility in business structure
- Plan and evaluate/Finding time
- Good business relationships
- Being proactive and persevering
- Ability to balance home and work.

Getting and taking advice

'I agree with Vincent's assessment of the situation: the biggest thing he did not do was to take advice. He needed a financial adviser from the start, and a good one, not just an accountant with an opinion. He may well have needed different advisers to deal with investors and with administration, but they are all out there if you look. They would have assessed the financial viability of XRZ and Hugan Investments in particular, and if they did not prevent the first disaster, they would surely have averted the second.'

A financial feel for the business

'In taking advice, Vincent would have learned much about the financial side of the business that he needed to know. Learning by making mistakes is a very risky and expensive way to acquire financial knowledge in business!'

Flexibility in business structure

'Vincent relied heavily on investors from the start, which was the root of his problem, and I have to ask why he decided to set up his business on what appears to have been a grand scale? He could have started smaller, grown steadily, and had far less financial exposure at the beginning. Again, good financial advice would have enabled him to build a less vulnerable structure.'

Plan and evaluate

'Failure to anticipate was a very big mistake. Vincent could see disaster coming, so what did he do? Just worked harder! Somewhere inside us there seems to be a belief that if we just do a good job, it will fend off bad things happening to us. Axilia demonstrates very clearly how you can run a business well, and yet still fail.

'Vincent needed a disaster avoidance plan, formed with an expert on administration. This would have either saved Axilia or prepared him for the negotiation that he eventually faced, and enabled him to seek alternative funding over days and weeks rather than in hours. He could easily have found the time for this, but he chose to spend it with his head down, busy delivering instead of facing the problem squarely.'

Good business relationships

'Vincent does not have a business buddy – someone to talk things over with. Investors can sometimes provide useful input, but obviously not in this case. A buddy might not have had any special expertise, but might have suggested to Vincent that he seek some.

'Vincent benefited in the end from a good business network, and from being a good networker by offering help with no immediate expectation of a return. This case demonstrates how well this networking policy can pay off.'

Being proactive and persevering

'Vincent has both these qualities, which he applied very successfully within his business, but not outside it, where he needed to be totally proactive in his management of investors, banks and funding.'

Ability to balance home and work

'Vincent is a shining example here, and clearly demonstrates how well you can cope if you are physically fit, and have a supportive home environment. You may not believe that physical fitness affects your business performance, but fitness is itself an achievement. When you feel you have achieved in one area, it is easier to believe that you can achieve in another. In a way, the physical facts are irrelevant, it is what you believe about them that matters.'

Your health check

Key questions to ask:

1 Am I happy with my work/home balance?
2 Do I have a business buddy to discuss things with?
3 Do I face up to likely problems, or keep my head down and hope they go away?
4 What do the words profit and cash mean in my business?
5 Do I have a contingency plan for emergencies?
6 How do I manage the relationship with investors? (If I have any)
7 Faced with unfamiliar territory, do I seek advice or wing it?

05

loss of focus

There are many reasons why you lose focus when running a company, and this chapter illustrates a particularly tragic one. However, even without the sad events described here, for this business there was already a need to take stock of where it was going, and the tragedy precipitated this. Therefore, this story shows that it does not take a catastrophe to make you lose focus, or to realize that you have lost it.

Company profile: Domane Interiors

Ben and Ashley were 'best mates' at college in the north of England, studying furniture design. They found jobs, stayed in touch, and were asked by a friend for some help with the furnishing and decor of a new barn conversion. They took him to London to buy furniture, and the job was a success. Afterwards, they realized that there was nowhere in Leeds to buy modern furniture, so they had the idea of setting up a furniture shop together.

Ben and Ashley managed to find some cheap premises and, with small loans from their families, they bought some stock and opened a small shop. It went well, they repaid the loans, having a policy of never borrowing and always having cash in the bank to cover any problems such as clients declaring bankruptcy and not paying them.

They moved to bigger and better premises, expanded the range, and decided to open another shop. Ben and Ashley took very little out of the business – 'just pocket money' – and reinvested all the time. Ashley wanted to get on to the property ladder and buy a house, but he continued to put the business first. After five years, they had saved up enough to afford another shop, so they found a nice premises in Harrogate, and went on a buying trip to Italy to choose some new lines. As with everything else that involved the business, it was fun and enjoyable for them both: 'We loved every minute – we had a real passion for what we were doing.'

It was at this point that disaster struck. Ben was woken at 2 a.m. to be told that Ashley had fallen from the balcony of his hotel room and had been taken to hospital. The hotel owner took Ben there, and he saw Ashley to speak to briefly, looking battered and with a broken arm, but nothing worse.

Ben said, 'For some time there was a great deal of activity in Ashley's room, then it stopped and the atmosphere changed. A policeman came to speak to me, and I could tell by the look in his eyes what he was going to say. He spoke very little English, but he told me that Ashley had died. It didn't seem possible. I rang my girlfriend's mother, who spoke fluent Italian, and asked her to talk to a doctor. She confirmed that Ashley died of internal injuries.'

Ben was distraught, and could not believe what had happened. He returned to England in a daze. His response was to take refuge in work. The owners of the Harrogate premises were very understanding, and told him he could pull out of the deal without any penalties. 'But I said no, I wanted to do it. It was mentally useful for me. I ought not to have neglected the business in Leeds, but I needed to do something else.' Ben put all his efforts into preparing the new shop in Harrogate, leaving his assistant, Susie, to run the Leeds shop.

Ben and Ashley had planned to open the Harrogate shop at the beginning of December, but it took Ben much longer to get the shop ready on his own, and it did not open until January. However, they had ordered all the furniture to arrive during November, ready for the opening, which meant that it had to be paid for at the end of December. They had expected to make some December sales to cover at least part of the costs, but that was obviously not going to happen. Apart from working very long hours, Ben also spent a great deal of time in the pub, trying to block out some of the nightmare he had experienced.

Consequently, it was January when stark reality hit Ben hard. 'I took my eye off the ball from September to January. Sales were declining in Leeds – I didn't realize the contribution I made to the place until I stopped doing it. All of a sudden all the invoices fell due. I owed £40,000 and had nothing in the bank and a pile of threatening letters. I hate getting pestered; I always pay people straightaway. It was horrendous.'

Ben and Ashley had always taken lots of advice about their business, and now Ben turned to his family, a number of whom specialized in insolvency: 'I knew that I could have gone bankrupt, stuffed all my suppliers and started up again with a new name. I knew exactly how to do it, but I did not want to let everyone down, so with my brother's help (he is an insolvency solicitor) I drafted a letter to the 20 companies I owed money to, explaining the circumstances, and asking for continued supply and proposing a planned repayment scheme, in order to avoid bankruptcy. Nineteen out of the 20 agreed.

'Then I had a horrible year, prioritizing how much to pay which supplier for what, in order to get stock in and keep on trading to pay off the debt. Before, the business was a passion – now it's hard work.'

Twelve months later, all the debts are paid, but Ben is far from happy: 'I've got to the point where we've got two shops and I wish we only had one. We have doubled our overheads, but not our customer base. I've had no time to focus over the past year. I want to re-evaluate what I want to do. I want to get more enjoyment out of the business, because the worst thing of all is my loss of enthusiasm, I've never felt like this before. It took an event like this to push me to take stock.

'Ashley and I were getting to the point where we would have done that anyway. We knew it would be a slog for the first three or four years, but after that we expected it to be easier, and to be able to pay ourselves a reasonable amount, but it didn't get any easier, and without Ashley it's obviously been much harder.'

Susie left, and Ashley took on Sally two months after Ashley died. Whereas Susie was an office administrator, Sally had taken the same course as Ben and Ashley and 'is more creative, more on our wavelength. I realize now that Susie was not the right person for the job. She told me that she did not like working on her own, and preferred to have regular guidance. In those circumstances she performed well and enjoyed what she did. I realize now that I left her alone all that time I was in Harrogate, and gave her little direction. It is hardly surprising that sales declined, and it wasn't her fault at all. I should have recognized the qualities we needed, which I believe I've now found in Sally. I pay her more than me, which isn't a lot, and I now want to set something up that will last.

'I'm going to close the shop in Leeds, and make a fresh start in Harrogate. There will be two of us there, and I'm going to spend a third of my time exploring what makes me happy and what makes Sally happy too. I want to find my excitement for my work again.'

Lessons learned

When Helen, the company doctor, talked to Ben, Ben was very clear that he and Ashley had made a number of mistakes.

'I think we were too careful with money. We only took on very cheap premises in Leeds, and they were not in main shopping streets. We should have borrowed a bit and gone for better locations. Our focus was on not being in debt, rather than getting ourselves into a position to generate higher volume sales.

'We also took on the Harrogate shop for the wrong reasons. We were too focused on visible expansion, which means expensive overheads, but it was the attractive route to take. In retrospect we should have developed the business much more from a single base, before expanding geographically. We had set up a website, and created some packaged offerings. We could have done far more on those, and on other activities to develop the business from one location.

'We did not focus enough on what we wanted from the business. Ashley could not afford to buy a house, yet we used all our money to set up Harrogate. If we had thought this through, we would have recognized that unless we changed something radically, Harrogate would not deliver any differently from Leeds, and would take a while to do even that, so our 'pocket money' would not increase for some time.

'We weren't clear what we wanted from Susie, and consequently we took on a square peg to fit into a pretty round hole, which became even more round when I spent all my time in Harrogate.

'I obviously lost focus after Ashley passed away. I can see now that I buried myself in the new work in Harrogate, staying away from Leeds, where there was more to remind me of the past. It was my way of coping personally, but I did not see, or want to see, what was happening to the business. I really needed a good friend who knew the business to help me see what I was doing, and take action in Leeds before it was too late. I didn't have anyone who fitted that description – of course I didn't, because I'd lost him in Italy.

'Now I find I've lost my passion for the business, and I know I have to get that back for Domane to really fly. What I am very focused on now is finding that enjoyment and passion again, both for me and for the business.'

Success tactics

Here is a summary of Helen's conclusions, which fall under the following headings:

- Getting and taking advice
- Plan and evaluate

- A clear focus
- Being proactive and persevering
- Commitment to business success
- Getting the best from your people
- A passion for what you do
- Ability to balance home and work.

Getting and taking advice

'I am full of admiration for Ben's ability to survive in the most difficult situation, where he was coping with his personal grief as well as running the business single-handed. It was at this time that he most needed advice and a sounding board, and of course it is obvious why he no longer had anyone close to the business to turn to.

'If he had been able to ask for help, both on the personal and the business front, his financial crisis could have been avoided, or at least minimized. Unfortunately, it is often at times when we most need help that we do not think of asking, or do not want to ask for it, but if he had, it would not have taken a great deal of business expertise to diagnose the problem and offer solutions.'

Plan and evaluate

'It is completely understandable that Ben did not plan or evaluate after Ashley's death. However, as he points out himself, he and Ashley were not really taking stock of their operation before the accident happened. They did not fully evaluate the Harrogate decision, particularly its impact on business overheads and the fact that it would mean that they would continue to pay themselves pocket money. They had already begun to develop the business in different ways, from a lower cost base, but instead of building on this they set off in a new and much more expensive direction.'

A clear focus

'By expanding to Harrogate, Ben and Ashley's focus was on visible expansion – the prestige of a second outlet. They told themselves they were doing it to grow the business and make more money, but a really close examination of the facts would have told a different story. If they had done this, they could then have weighed up their conflicting goals – earning more, increasing sales, and having a new shop. With this view, they could then have decided exactly what their focus was to be.'

Being proactive and persevering/Commitment to business success

'There is absolutely no lack of these qualities in Domane, and this is what has enabled Ben to survive so well. He is rightly concerned now whether he will be able to continue in this way in the future, and he is absolutely right to ask this question. Having put so much of himself into the business, and found it such hard work, is he now in danger of losing commitment, and the staying power that has seen him through all his difficulties? Spending a third of his time in dealing with this issue is critical to the future, for Ben himself, and for the business.'

Getting the best from your people

'Susie was recruited at a time when her office skills mattered more than her proactive selling skills, but still Ben recognized, and indeed Susie told him, that she was not in the right job. When everything changed, this became critical, and if Ben had had the right person in Leeds, his financial difficulties would have been much reduced, and in fact he or she might have done more to alert him to the problems that were building up.

'This is a very sad illustration of how vital it is to be clear on the personal qualities you want from an employee, and to really think through the job they will be doing, and the skills they need to do it.'

A passion for what you do

'Ben recognizes that his passion is no longer there, or at least that he cannot feel it now, which may not be the same thing. He is right in thinking that this is crucial to the future of the business, and dedicating a significant proportion of his time to finding it again is an excellent plan.'

Ability to balance home and work

'Domane is a rare example of a successful mix of business and friendship, and the balance between home and work was not really an issue for Ben or Ashley because work was fun, and they were friends, so 'too much work' did not really apply to them.

'Ben alone, however, found that work had become 'hard work' and he did not enjoy it, so the question of finding a balance now arises. Ben's overwork was therapeutic for a while, but now that he is engaged to be married, this situation has changed, and part of finding his passion and enjoyment for the business will also need to involve finding the right balance of work and home life.'

Conclusion

'As a final point, I would like to commend Ben, not just for his perseverance in seeing this through, but also in resisting the temptation to go bankrupt, which was the obvious option. He is a shining example of someone in business with true loyalty not just to his clients but also to his suppliers; someone who acted with complete integrity and courage, at a time when he had the perfect excuse for taking the easy way out.'

Your health check

Key questions to ask:

1 How clear is the focus of my business to me?
2 How well do I define the focus of my business to others and to myself?
3 Do I have a written plan to achieve the focus of my business?
4 Is my caution holding the business back?
5 If my business involves premises, have I invested in the right location?
6 How do I ensure that I define jobs accurately, and then find the right people to fit them?
7 How can I maintain or enhance my passion for the business?

06

sales too low

When you are well established and have a track record of success, it can take a long time to recognize that your market is no longer what it was, and that you need to take some serious action just to maintain your sales. It is easy to blame other things, which often come disguised as your problem, when poor sales are really the root of it. The company in this chapter hit the wall and just managed to bounce back.

Company profile: Fennymall Sandstone Ltd

Jeff and Harry are brothers who have been running Brody Quarries, the family sandstone business for many years. They are based in the Peak District in England, and have always supplied the building trade in the region. There are many Grade I and Grade II listed buildings in the area, and this was the core of their business. They employ about ten people – mostly skilled craftsmen – and traded in the way that they had always traded until two things happened.

First, there was a gradual decline in the market, which had been going on for some time. Jeff and Harry had seen competitors close their quarries, but they had survived largely because of their good reputation both as a business and for the quality of their product and their workmanship. Now their sales were dropping too.

Second, there was an event that was catastrophic when combined with the decline in the market. A client refused to pay a bill for £50,000. Despite all their efforts, they could get nothing from this very large organization, and they did not have the time or the funds to pursue them through the courts, which would have probably taken about two years. With much reduced sales and a heavy overdraft, Jeff and Harry could see no way out, so they called in Alan, a company doctor, to do what he described as a 'phoenix operation' on the business.

Alan told them first to talk to their landlord, since he could 'pull the plug' on them overnight and close them down if he chose to. With Jeff and Harry's excellent track record, the landlord agreed to wait for his rent. Alan then advised that one of the two directors would need to go bankrupt and, after some discussion, they simply tossed a coin: Jeff called heads, and lost. Before the bankruptcy was declared, they talked to their key small suppliers. They explained that they were being forced into bankruptcy, but while this meant that it would wipe out all their debts, they would do their best to pay them generously for new orders when they started up as a new company. These were off-the-record conversations between trusted business colleagues, and they served to preserve the great goodwill that Brody had built up over the years.

The staff were also told what was happening and why. They knew that the new company would re-employ them all and so, when the bankruptcy was announced, it created the minimum ill will possible in what is a very tight business community, with the larger suppliers and the bank taking the brunt of the impact.

Jack Brody was Harry's eldest son, and not connected with the business at all. He agreed to set up a new business entity with a new name, Fennymall Sandstone Ltd, with his father and uncle as shareholders, responsible for running the firm as before. He opened a new bank account with a different bank. Jeff and Harry re-employed the staff, and it was business as usual, except that the underlying problem had not yet been addressed.

Alan then took steps to reverse the sales decline by finding two people to help the company, both part-time, and both self-employed. Jim had been a sandstone distributor all his life. He had retired, but had got bored, so was delighted to work on a part-time basis, finding new clients for Fennymall. They now supply sandstone flooring to some companies in London and Bristol which sell very upmarket kitchens. Fennymall are also supplying sandstone to specialized builders who are constructing large houses in the old style, using traditional materials, and to a company that is creating garden seating out of sandstone. Ashley specializes in marketing and, working just two days a week, he has helped them to set up a showroom in what was an overflow stock room. He followed this up by advertising in local upmarket magazines, such as *Derbyshire Life*, so now there is a steady stream of direct sales for Fennymall.

Last year, Jeff and Harry agreed that they could each take a holiday for the first time in ten years.

Lessons learned

Harry and Jeff were not entirely happy about some of the lessons they had learned. Harry said, 'We realize we're a bit old-fashioned when it comes to honouring a commitment. This experience has taught us not to trust our clients, which is sad, but practical. We've also learned to be tough about payment terms, and to be prepared to walk away if the cash implications look too risky. It has been a nice surprise to see how clients are prepared to negotiate, once they know you are serious.'

Jeff's comment was: 'It's all so easy with hindsight, isn't it? We can see all the problems now, and what we should have done, but at the time you're too involved, too busy trying to keep the wheel turning. We make a real effort now to stand back and take stock, but it's hard when there's so much to do, just to keep going with business as usual. You can really sum up our problem as this: we didn't know what we didn't know, and that included not knowing that we needed advice, until we were forced into it.

'Now we know, we make full use of our advisers, and they act as a discipline for us because they force us to stand back and review and plan. Even after all we've been through, I'm not convinced we'd manage it on our own, but happily we don't have to, and nor does anyone else, if they take time to think about things.'

Success tactics

Alan's comments fall under the following headings:

- To lead or to manage the business
- A feel for the market
- Management controls
- Plan and evaluate
- Getting and taking advice
- Being proactive and persevering
- Good business relationships
- A passion for what you do.

To lead or to manage the business

'Jeff and Harry have clearly done both leading and managing successfully in the past. It is evident that the world moved on, and Jeff and Harry ceased to provide the leadership that their company needed – they did not focus on change or create a new vision for Brody.'

A feel for the market

'A feel for the market is the key to Fennymall's future success. Jeff and Harry understood their old market well and could see that it was declining, but they did not know how to find new markets. They had never needed to learn, and they had the vague notion that marketing just meant advertising and they could not see the point of that since they were a supplier to other businesses that knew them anyway. They needed both market and marketing expertise to take them forward, and their problem was not that they lacked these skills, but that they failed to seek them out.'

Management controls

'It is easy with hindsight to tell small companies not to trust their large clients when it comes to paying bills, because at the time of the order everyone is thrilled to win such a large piece of business. Different payment terms could have made all the difference to Brody, combined with a really tight credit control process, to ensure that payment history is monitored and that bills are paid on time.'

Plan and evaluate

'If Jeff and Harry had sat down and projected their sales figures a year ahead, and then built in some possible glitches in cash flow, that would have provoked them to do something, even without the loss of £50,000. Instead they did what so many of us do, they carried on and worked even harder at what they had, hoping that it would all come right in the end.'

Getting and taking advice

'Now Jeff and Harry know that they should have found advice earlier, as soon as sales started to dip, to bring in the market expertise they were lacking. It was unfortunate that it took a cash problem to illuminate what was really going wrong in the business, but they did then seek the advice they needed, and invested in new markets.'

Being proactive and persevering

'Jeff and Harry made great efforts to keep sales going with their existing customer base, but they were not proactive in seeking new markets, nor in finding any help to do this, until it was too late for Brody.'

Good business relationships

'Jeff and Harry have excellent business relationships with staff, suppliers and clients, which is what has enabled them to continue in the sandstone business. However, they were not using those relationships. They could probably have found Jim, if they'd tried and asked around. They might have obtained some free help with marketing or an introduction or two. They are delighted with Jim and Ashley's contribution, but they came too late to save Brody.'

A passion for what you do

'Sometimes declining sales are caused by a loss of enthusiasm for your product or service. This was clearly not the case with Brody. Jeff and Harry love the sandstone business – it is all they know. The problem was that their passion was only directed at their old client base. Now, when Jim or Ashley presents them with a prospect, Jeff and Harry often win the prospect over with their passion for their high-quality products.'

Your health check

Key questions to ask:

1 Am I providing business leadership and vision for now and for the future?
2 What are the trends in my market?
3 What can I do to capitalize on the trends?
4 Am I using the best resources in the best way to win sales?
5 How tight is my credit control process?
6 Do I need help with:
   a Market analysis
   b Marketing
   c Sales?

07 quality of service

When your business is built on quality of personal service, expansion presents a particular challenge. In this chapter, we see what happens when a company hires new people who do not deliver the same quality of service as the owners. The irony is that the owners are 'people people' and should be the experts, but instead they fall into all the obvious traps, not least that of failing to define precisely what it is that their clients are buying from them. Without this information, it is unlikely that they will identify the right qualities in job applicants.

Company profile: Ronaldson Rey

The company that fell into the service quality trap was a small training partnership called Ronaldson Rey, which had been set up five years before by Jeff Ronaldson and Barry Rey. Jeff and Barry had worked together in a large multinational company, and were both trainers. Barry majored on skills in managing staff performance, and Jeff did sales training. One day, as they were sitting in the canteen discussing the managing director's new car, Jeff suggested that they go it alone. 'What chance do we stand of owning a car like that if we stay here?'

Jeff and Barry went into things quite carefully, and were debating when to take the plunge and resign, when they had a huge stroke of luck. The company announced a major downsizing programme and asked for volunteers for redundancy. The training department was a prime target for redundancies, so Jeff and Barry were not only first in the queue, but they also told the company that they would happily provide their training services in future as consultants.

The two worked well as a partnership. Jeff was the front man, a natural performer, and an excellent salesman. Barry was a thorough, detail man. He dealt with the finance, the bookings, the course materials, as well as running his performance review courses. His style was very different from Jeff's, but he was a quietly confident presenter and very perceptive. He had plenty of experience of managing people, and the skills of handling an appraisal or performance review were ones he could easily demonstrate to his trainees; through applying the very skills he was teaching, Barry could give them excellent feedback on their performance in the training room.

Soon Jeff and Barry were both delivering training every week, sometimes five days a week. They sat down one day and agreed that they were both getting very tired, and that they were in danger of turning business away because they could not cope.

'We shall have to take on some staff,' Jeff said.

'We could just subcontract the work to other independent trainers like Allison or Nigel and make them associates,' Barry countered.

'And then they'll steal our clients.'

'All right then, if we're going to hire, who shall we hire? Someone experienced and expensive, or someone young and cheap? You know that having employees is a big deal for a small business like ours, and there are lots more costs than just the salary.'

Jeff and Barry agreed to think it over, and identify candidates from their network of contacts. Having looked at the total cost of employing someone senior, they agreed that two juniors would make much more sense. They could train them to do things the Ronaldson Rey way, and they would ensure consistency of service. The search took a long time, and they were desperate by the time they found Amy and Garth. Garth had been a salesman for 18 months, and Jeff knew him through a friend of a friend. He was young, confident and full of enthusiasm. Barry saw another Jeff in the making and, though he didn't really take to Garth personally, he decided that it was good discipline to choose the individual for their skills and not for personal reasons, and anyway they were desperate so he did not say anything to Jeff.

Jeff, on the other hand, had lots of doubts about Amy before he met her. 'She's not had much experience, Barry. I know you say she managed a café while she was a student, but that doesn't amount to much.'

'You haven't read her details properly. She's been a team leader in this telesales operation as well. But you wait until you see her.'

Amy was full of confidence and enthusiasm. She had been selected as in-house trainer in the call centre, and loved it. Jeff was won over: 'Great personality, Barry. I see now why you chose her. She's really passionate about training.'

Barry arranged for Amy and Garth to join at the same time, and had planned a free week to teach them all the basics. This was hard to do, as he was under so much pressure, but he told himself it was worth the investment. Then he started getting chest pains, and was whisked into hospital the night before Amy and Garth started work. Jeff did what he could, which was not a lot, as he was training in Warrington from Tuesday to Friday. On Friday Barry was sent home from hospital with an uncertain verdict on his health. It was probably not a heart attack, it was probably stress, but whichever it was, he needed to take it easy.

Amy and Garth were plunged in at the deep end and, being the people they were, they coped by appearing confident and enthusiastic, no matter what. This seemed to work, and Jeff and Barry were relieved and delighted to find that the two of them came back from courses full of success stories, and with pretty good feedback from the delegates. As time went on, however, the danger signals began to appear.

Barry received a call from Angela, his assistant. Their biggest client wanted a new series of appraisal courses running – by Barry. 'They said they wanted you. I said Amy was available, and they said no, it had to be you.'

Barry called the client who said, 'Amy's a lovely girl, Barry, but she just doesn't have the depth of management experience, and it shows.'

That evening, Barry discussed the situation with Jeff, who said, 'Well, I'll resist saying I told you so Barry, because I'm having similar problems with Garth. He's a great performer, the delegates find him very entertaining, but he's not very interested in their performance and he skimps on the exercises, so I learned from a mate of mine who just happens to work with someone Garth trained last week. He said that Garth just left them to it for the exercises, and the feedback sessions were superficial. The only time Garth really engaged with them was in looking at the videos of the final sales exercise, then he'd make jokes about people. Some can take it and some can't, but because of Garth's style, it's not the done thing to object and quite a few people left feeling humiliated and less confident than when they started. This chap was one of those, and I won't tell you what he called Garth.'

'And what does Garth say?'

'I haven't spoken to him yet. I'm trying to calm down, and I wanted your views anyway, because I'd like to fire him.'

'And replace him with…?'

'Dunno – I'm still thinking. Now you've told me about Amy, looks like there aren't too many options.'

A long discussion followed, and Jeff and Barry reached a number of painful conclusions. Amy could train only junior managers, and they would have to find an associate to help Barry out, and to give Barry time to train Amy. Jeff would speak to Garth immediately and get to the root of the problem, which might be fixable. Barry would help with this, if Jeff lost patience.

They put the plan into action, spurred on by a call to Jeff, the next day, from a new client who had had a complaint from one of the female delegates about the way she was treated on the sales course. This gave him the ammunition he needed to speak to Garth, who was obviously shocked but then tried to laugh it off. In the end, Jeff got through to him by videoing a sales demonstration that he made Garth do with Barry. Jeff then gave Garth a taste of his own medicine by a vicious, but funny critique: 'And think, Garth, there's only Barry to hear this. Imagine if all your mates were listening.'

On the management training side, Barry knew that Allison was the right associate to help him out. Mature and well respected for her management experience, she performed well in the training room and carried the reputation of Ronaldson Rey with ease. This gave him time to spend with a distraught Amy, who believed she had done such a good job, and that the older delegates just complained because of her age. Barry persevered but had trouble getting through to her, and in the end realized that she just did not know how much she did not know, despite his efforts to enlighten her.

One evening, Jeff said, 'Barry, you're looking more tired than ever, and Amy is clearly not happy. Why don't you just call it a day and stick with Allison? – that seems to be working really well.'

'I'm glad you said that, Jeff, because I've just been thinking about the business, and actually I'm not sure I want the hassle of staff or of growing much bigger than we are. Quality control of trainers in the training room is a nightmare, and if we arranged things a bit differently, we could have a really good lifestyle as we are.'

'Well, it wouldn't surprise me if Garth doesn't leave in a while. I recognize the signs. Perhaps we won't replace him either. I don't really want to use an associate, but if I just control my diary tightly and say no, then I can probably put my prices up anyway, so yes, I'm with you, growth isn't everything – let's choose our clients and stop worrying about all that business out there!'

Barry was not sure that Jeff could really be happy without growing, but for now they were in agreement. He came to an amicable arrangement with Amy, and with her departure he and Jeff heaved a joint sigh of relief. Provided they kept an eye on Garth, they were now confident of providing the same quality of service on which they had built their business.

Lessons learned

Alan, the company doctor, was delighted to see that not only did Jeff and Barry recognize all their mistakes, they also took complete responsibility for them and could see what they should have done, which is not always the case.

Jeff said, 'We didn't plan our expansion. We just set up, got busy, couldn't cope, and started looking for people. If we'd thought about it at the beginning, we might not have wanted to expand at all, and might have adopted a different strategy, like doing less training for higher fees.

'We also didn't instil in the new people our company values, and our passion for customer service. These are things that Barry and I take for granted, so we didn't think to say them.

'I think we should have got professional help, or at least advice, about recruiting. In the end, we got so desperate we were close to hiring anything that moved. It was a false economy to do it ourselves and we were also trying to save money on salaries too – a very expensive mistake.

Barry said, 'I lost sight of my market. Amy's experience of management was enough, with my help, to enable her to train first-line supervisors, whereas I'd been training middle to senior managers, and that's where I needed the expertise.

'We hadn't properly planned the training for Amy and Garth. They really needed lots of joint training time, and we just couldn't cope with that, we needed them out there delivering, and that tripped us up very badly indeed. If we'd really managed and mentored them properly, we would never have had those complaints.

'We realized how poor our contact with our clients really is. You collect a few happy sheets from a course, and you think you have a measure of the training. By the time a client works up to complaining, it's probably too late.'

Success tactics

Here is a summary of Alan's conclusions, which fall under the following headings:

- Plan and evaluate
- Finding time
- A passion for what you do
- A feel for the market
- Good business relationships
- Getting the best from your people
- Getting and taking advice.

Plan and evaluate

'If Jeff and Barry had stopped to think, their planning would have been as follows:

1 The future of the business.
2 How to get there – if by expansion, then:
   a Definition of services offered – what do our clients buy from us?
   b Definition of new roles.
   c Definition of selection criteria: personal qualities and skills needed.
   d Recruitment plan – who to do it, how and when.
   e Training plan – who to do it, how and when.

'As is obvious to them now, Jeff and Barry missed this vital and lengthy stage of the process, which would have transformed the outcome of whatever route they took for the future. If they had decided to recruit, they would be so clear about what they wanted that the thought of taking on someone who did not fit, in pure desperation, would not have been an option.'

Finding time

If they had taken the time to plan, Jeff and Barry would not have found themselves rushed off their feet – literally, in Barry's case. This is the perfect illustration of poor time management. It led to increasing problems – no time to do a good recruitment job, no time to train Garth and Amy, no time to talk to customers – no time to do anything except worry and deliver instead of thinking and planning. Jeff and Barry fell into the classic small business trap.

A passion for what you do

'Jeff and Barry had this: it was why they were successful, and they did look for passion in their new recruits. However, they mistook a passion for performing, which was what Garth and Amy had, for a passion for customer service, which they did not have. A much clearer analysis of what clients were buying was needed, and then it would have been easier to test for the relevant skills and qualities in the selection process. Given the right recruits, Jeff and Barry then needed to invest a lot of time instilling their customer service values and passion in their staff.'

A feel for the market

'Barry obviously knew his market was middle to senior management, but he lost sight of it in his desperation to hire some help which, in hindsight, looks difficult to believe. In reality, this is a perfect illustration of how too much pressure can stop you thinking straight, and how vital it is to stand back and take stock.'

Good relationships

'Jeff and Barry were in danger of taking their client relationships for granted, and managed to rescue them just in time. This is the most dangerous position to be in with a client, when you think you have nothing to worry about and cease to be vigilant in looking for signs of dissatisfaction or change.

'Barry also observed that they should cultivate better relationships with other associates, 'as you never know when you might need one!''

Getting the best from your people

'I'll let Barry comment on this section, as it is his speciality:

"We would do everything differently here! Analyse the role, pin down the specification, and get the right person in. Then attune their values and vision to ours, set standards and clear expectations, train them thoroughly. Assess their performance, and give them lots of feedback, good and bad, but hopefully lots of good. Check carefully on client reactions, and reward them in line with performance. We didn't get past the first hurdle, and we feel particularly bad about this, because it's all in our training courses!"

'Clearly they both know all this backwards, but it demonstrates again how easy it is to stop thinking when you feel you have to keep running.'

Getting and taking advice

Jeff and Barry both felt that if they had given themselves time to think and plan, they could have worked out most of the answers for themselves, without advice. They probably did not need an adviser to work out what they both wanted from the business, but an outsider might have prompted the discussion by asking some basic questions, like: 'Are you sure this is what you want?' or 'Aren't you driving yourselves too hard?' This would have helped Jeff and Barry to stand back and take stock, which would have given them the perspective they needed.

'They recognize that some professional help with recruitment would have taken the pressure off, and would also have forced them to think harder about who they were looking for, and to be more stringent in their selection process.'

Conclusion

Jeff and Barry are both skilled in many aspects of business management, and if a client came to them with the Ronaldson Rey problem, they would no doubt give better textbook answers than I could. The fact that they made almost every mistake in that same book does show how hard it can be to see the wood when you are deep in the trees; even when you do know all the answers, and know how valuable an outsider can be as a catalyst to stop you running and start you thinking again.'

Your health check

Key questions to ask:

1 What do I want from my business?
2 How well do I communicate this to everyone involved?
3 How do I plan the use of my time?
4 What exactly do my customers buy from me?
5 How do I ensure that my staff share my passion?
6 How do I define the roles of my staff?
7 How do they know what I expect of them?
8 What external expertise do I call upon to help make my business a success?

08

market changes

When your business is thriving and you are struggling to keep up with demand, it takes a great deal of self-discipline to stand back and check on market trends. Markets are dynamic, and if your company does not track change then you may be left behind or, as in this case, your market may disappear.

Company profile: Crozby Dezign

Danielle Crozby left university with a degree in graphic design, and three years later she had set up her own agency. Here, she tells her story:

'It was a bit early to do that, looking back now, but the market was buoyant and my agency grew quite quickly. I won new clients easily, and I built up a design team until I had four designers, an administrative assistant and an account executive, who looked after existing clients.

'I made all the classic mistakes, chasing revenue rather than profit, but the economy was booming, and it was relatively easy to succeed. I hired the designers straight from college. I made contacts there and made sure I got the good ones but, of course, I had to continue their training, and I didn't put too much pressure on them. I knew the difference between being a designer at college and a designer in the commercial world, and the pace at which they operate is very different. I let them be designers as they had come to understand the word, which I knew was important to them, but the trade-off was a big loss in efficiency, which I chose to swallow. All this meant that my margins were not great, but we were making a profit, and I didn't pay a lot of attention to margin at that time.

'Then three things happened. My long-term boyfriend, who I'd lived with since college, went off with someone else. I should have seen it coming, but I didn't, and it threw me. The next thing to throw me was the economy, which took a sudden nose-dive. Design and publicity budgets were the first to go, and our sales went through the floor. That was bad enough, but the last horror was the worst, and it happened at the same time – computers hit the design industry. This meant there were Apple Macintosh computers everywhere and, instead of designers, companies were employing Mac operators. This trend was exacerbated by the flood of designers coming from the new university courses. When I graduated, there were really only two good courses to choose from, now there is a myriad selection, all feeding the Mac operator role. Because this essentially deskilled design, printers moved into this area, and in some cases were offering design for free in order to maintain their print business.

'Of course, this didn't all happen instantly, but it didn't take long to feel the effects, and I had to remortgage my house to keep things going. We had to buy the Macs in too, to keep up, and this meant that my designers were no longer doing the work they loved. It was a blessing really because they left one by one, which saved me having to lay them off as sales declined. So all my staff went, and I was left alone behind the drawing board, or rather behind the Mac. I'd left my premises, and started working from home. I met my present husband, who's a freelance writer, and I had enough residual business to bring in a reasonable income. Nothing fantastic, but I was suddenly released from the pressure of paying rent and salaries, and with minimal overheads I could manage very well. I decided that I didn't want to employ anyone else again – working to pay other people's mortgages is a permanent pressure I can do without.

'So, having started out in the business of selling artistic talent, I was now more of a computer operator. Like my designers, I did not warm to this change of role, which technology had deskilled, and although I continued doing it, my heart was not in it.

'Part of the essence of design is creative thinking, and so, faced with mundane work my brain ticked away, looking for a way out. If I could sell something which I designed myself, to my own specification and not to other people's, that would satisfy some of my compromised standards. I started to think of all the things that I could design and sell, and I came up with the idea of my own range of wrapping paper for men.

'I have a great relationship with a couple of printers, and we work in collaboration. They are what I find to be increasingly rare in business these days – people who keep their word and who are reliable. They give me a price and then stick to it – that is unusual, in my experience.

'Holding stock is a bit of a challenge, but we have a very large garage and that's been big enough so far. I've had great success with specialist stationery groups, and Internet sales are doing nicely too. I'm going to expand into wine bottle gift boxes, which are a frequent gift for men, and I have some definite interest in those. My designs are original, and very appealing to women who buy for men – I think that's the secret.

'Obviously it's been a big shift to move from selling services to selling a product, and I will have to grapple with inventory problems sooner or later – both volume and storage – I know that's a tightrope I have to walk. The big thing for me is that I'm back doing what I love – selling my own designs, which are not compromised by technology.'

Lessons learned

Danielle was very open about her business expertise with Alan, our company doctor: 'I think I've made every mistake in the book, but the worst one was not seeing the market change until it was too late. I was too busy running the business to think about market trends.

'I didn't think much about margins either and, in fact, I discovered that I made more profit on my own, working from home, than the agency did at its peak. If I'd really had my eye on the technology ball, I could have hired computer operators from the beginning, or else decided that wasn't a business I wanted to be in. As it was, I was just carried along on the wave of change, and fortunately I didn't quite drown on the way. The really important lesson I learned was to follow my passion. That's what has really worked for me.'

Success tactics

Alan's thoughts on Crozby Dezign fall under the following headings:

- A feel for the market
- A financial feel for the business
- Plan and evaluate
- Getting and taking advice.

A feel for the market

'Danielle has been remarkably successful in both her enterprises, but she is in danger of making the same mistake in stationery that she made in design. She paid little attention to the trends in the design market, and she shows no evidence of tracking trends in her new business area.

'Stationery is a completely new field for Danielle. She has relied on her design expertise so far, and it has proved successful, but she has done little research and is proposing to launch a new product range more on the basis of intuition than fact. She may be lucky again, but I would expect to see a more formal approach to assessing this market and, in doing this, she may even discover better opportunities.'

A financial feel for the business

'Danielle has developed this for the services business through hard experience, but I'm not sure she has it yet for a product sales operation. She has that general feeling of comfort which comes from not having any major business overheads by working from home, but that does not insulate you entirely from cash flow problems. If a major client cancels a big order at the last minute, and another delays payment, she could still find herself in difficulty. I would expect to see more formal controls and checks, particularly on cash.'

Plan and evaluate

Having looked at Danielle's current business figures, Alan has some concerns over structure, and most particularly inventory:

'I know Danielle is very conscious of this, but she's not being proactive about it. I would like to see her planning some scenarios of sales against purchases. There is a danger that she is buying high quantities to get low prices and to offer short lead times to her clients, but she is running the risk of building up high stocks that she might not sell and of hitting cash flow problems too.'

Getting and taking advice

'It would be really helpful for Danielle to find a business buddy who knows something about the stationery market – perhaps someone who sells complementary products – so that they could share ideas and experience.

'Or she could take some financial advice about inventory control, and consider where she might find some useful information about trends in the stationery market. All this should ensure that history does not repeat itself, and that she builds on her current success.'

Your health check

Key questions to ask:

1 How would I detect a decline in my market?
2 What would I do about it?
3 How would I create a market plan?
4 What resources could I call upon to make the market plan fly?
5 Do I really have a feel for how my business finances work?
6 If I keep inventory, do I understand the impact it can have on cash?

09

bad debt

You may be running your business very successfully, keeping tight control of costs, with a good revenue stream, when disaster strikes in the form of a bad debt. As this case study shows, often the culprit is well disguised, and gives no impression of being the financially insecure operator who will betray you and leave you with little or no redress.

Company profile: Lyne-Light

Lyne-Light is a thriving manufacturing company in the West Midlands in England. With only 12 employees, it has been the supplier of various types of welding equipment for 35 years to every kind of market, from the makers of decorative wrought iron to major car manufacturers. It has a very broad customer base numbering about 1500 active clients, buying anything from small welding torches to huge pieces of industrial equipment, worth £100,000 apiece.

Like many small companies, Lyne-Light finds it hard to deal with some of the large organizations, who can take advantage of their dominant market position, and demand very tough terms. To make matters worse, large organizations can also take a long time to pay their bills, and this is what led Lyne-Light into serious trouble.

A large client, who had purchased from Lyne-Light several times before, placed an order for a sizeable machine. The client was on normal terms of 30 days' payment, and Lyne-Light knew that they would get paid in 90, based on their previous track record. The machine was installed and operating successfully. Lyne-Light had sourced quite a high percentage of components as well as raw materials for this machine, and by now had paid its suppliers for these, since it maintained a policy of treating its suppliers as it would wish to be treated.

As the 90-day period came close to expiry, Lyne-Light started chasing the money, which amounted to over £20,000. As bad luck would have it, this came at a time when Lyne-Light had a lot of bills to pay, and not much coming in from their clients. The managing director, Robert Lyne, escalated the problem to the finance director in the client company, who explained that he was under instructions from their parent operation, and could do nothing right now, but would be able to very soon. This dialogue went on for a further three months, with a new and plausible reason for the delay as well as jam tomorrow offered every time, until one day Robert rang and was told that the finance director was no longer there, as the company was going into liquidation.

Robert had had dealings with official receivers before, and knew that there would be no hope of getting paid, and indeed little hope of getting his machine back. Having suffered before, Lyne-Light always put a reservation of title clause into their agreements, which states that the goods remain their property until fully paid for. They even print this on the back of their order acknowledgements. This did not carry any weight with the receiver, which would not release the machine and sold the company with its assets, including Lyne-Light's machine, to another large organization which was not liable for any outstanding debt.

If Lyne-Light were angry with the client who did not pay, they were even more angry with the receiver, but all their efforts failed and now they had a very serious cash flow problem. Their bank was in London, remote from them and lacking understanding of small businesses. This came about because Lyne-Light was purchased as a going concern, over 20 years ago, and the funding was obtained through a very good contact from a large merchant bank in the City. In all this time, no one from the bank had ever visited the company and, for the most part, contact had been limited to an annual meeting in the City. Initially, relations had been good but then the bank's staff changed and Lyne-Light had not rebuilt the relationship. It took many meetings and a great deal of blood, sweat and tears to get the bank to agree to extend the company's overdraft facility.

At the same time, Lyne-Light had to contact a number of its key suppliers, including their landlords, to explain the situation and ask for extended credit. Fortunately, Lyne-Light have an excellent reputation with their suppliers, established over many years, and the majority agreed to give them two or three months' grace, knowing them to be reliable and trustworthy. With their suppliers' help and the bank overdraft, Lyne-Light managed to survive, and two years later the company is in better shape than ever, with no bank overdraft at all, and a stringent policy on payment terms.

Lessons learned

Robert described to Alan, the company doctor, the action that Lyne-Light took after the crisis:

'We had always been careful about payment terms,' Robert commented, 'but after this happened, we decided to get much more rigorous. Any new organization, particularly a large one, is now asked to pay against a proforma invoice, which means we get 100 per cent up front. These companies often protest and tell us that, as a household name, we can rely on them, but we tell them that we are too small to take risks, which some of them accept. Others settle for 50 per cent up front and 50 per cent on delivery, but we are still far better off than we were with clients who paid at 90 days.

'We also keep a list of poor payers and, if they do it too often, we refuse to supply them. Sometimes they just go away, sometimes it bucks up their ideas, and they start paying properly. We still can't guarantee that it won't happen to us again, but we do all we can to prevent it, including maintaining a broad customer base so that we do not have too many eggs in one client's basket.

'The final thing we did was to manage our bank much more proactively. We have made a point of asking for overdraft extensions to cover specific situations, and then ensuring that they come well within the overdraft limit. Now we have a good track record of proactive financial management, and we have established good personal relationships there too.'

Success tactics

Here is a summary of Alan's suggestions for Lyne-Light, which fall under the following headings:

- Management controls
- Getting and taking advice
- Good business relationships
- Flexibility in business structure
- Being proactive and persevering.

Management controls

'Lyne-Light now have in place a tight set of controls for managing debt, which they have created from very bitter experience, and this does mean that they are far more likely to stick to them!

'It can be very difficult for small companies to argue with very large ones that are likely to go and take their business elsewhere.

As it discovered, however, Lyne-Light is in a strong position competitively, and its clients were far less likely to go elsewhere than it feared. It is important to know your strengths in order to negotiate effectively, and also to know how you would handle a bad debt, and whether you are prepared to walk away from an order – as Lyne-Light now are, which again strengthens their position.'

Getting and taking advice

'Lyne-Light had considered selling its invoices to a factoring agency, but felt the costs were too high. In deciding to do it themselves, the company could have taken some professional advice on debt collecting, because it was much too gentle in its approach. Lyne-Light spent six months trying to get money out of their client. A professional would almost certainly have managed to extract at least a part payment in that time.

'Similarly, Lyne-Light could have obtained professional advice and help on dealing with the receiver, especially as this was not the company's first bad experience of dealing with companies who have gone into liquidation.'

Good business relationships

Relationship with clients

'I have asked Lyne-Light whether they could have detected liquidation in the air when they visited their client, and they assured me that there were no signs of any problem. I accept that while this can be spotted in small to medium organizations, it can be difficult to detect in a large company, particularly one which belongs to a group. Often the staff themselves are unaware of the problem, and even the local management board might believe that they are getting group backing and be as surprised as Lyne-Light when the rug is pulled. Whatever the specifics of this case, it is vital to keep checking on your clients' financial status, which can be far from your mind when you are busy selling to them.'

Relationship with suppliers

'Lyne-Light's relationship with the bank left much to be desired, although there was clearly fault on both sides. Because the bank was so remote, and because of staff changes, Lyne-Light did not have a solid relationship on which to base its request for help, and the company has now taken steps to change that.

'Where Lyne-Light was really strong was in its relationship with its suppliers. The company had clearly built up a great deal of goodwill over the years and this investment paid off in a crisis, which is the real measure of the quality of a business relationship.'

Flexibility in business structure

'Lyne-Light achieved the flexibility it needed in this crisis with money from the bank and credit from its suppliers. It would be wise for the company to prepare a contingency plan to deal with another incident of this kind. Beyond Lyne-Light's bank and its suppliers, the company could examine how to shore up its finances in other ways, so that it is better able to withstand financial pressure. A supplement to the company's regular accounting advice would be an obvious next step.'

Being proactive and persevering

'Lyne-Light now has a very proactive system of credit control, and it has taken the initiative in its relationship with its bank, and in ensuring breadth in its customer base. Extending this approach to contingency planning will ensure that it minimizes the effect of this problem happening again.'

Your health check

Key questions to ask:

1 How would I cope with a very large bad debt?
2 Do I have a proactive credit control system?
3 Do I know when I am prepared to walk away from a client's order?
4 Do I track my clients' financial stability?
5 How would my bank respond to my needs in a crisis?
6 Do I have a contingency plan for emergencies?

10

external factors
– acts of God

Many things can happen to a business which are completely outside the owner's control: floods, terrorist attacks and economic collapse are just a few examples. In this case study, Carl's bolt from the blue was on a smaller scale, but its effect was major because it threw him into a catastrophic situation.

Company profile: Daniels Donovan

Carl Daniels was a chartered civil engineer, working for Abbots Newham, an engineering consulting group which was expanding rapidly across the UK. Carl had the chance to move to Abbots Newham's new Exeter office, and was soon promoted to partner. Then the company was taken over by E.K. Construction Ltd, and he found himself a director of his division, responsible for all of the south west of the country. His salary increased by 40 per cent, he had a very nice car, and lots of stock options in the group.

For five years things went wonderfully well – financially, at least. Carl bought a big new house and put his three children into private schools. He tried to resist the constant pressure from the group to move into commercial work when he had specialized in the public sector, but he was only partially successful and they did take on some commercial projects, about which he was not entirely comfortable.

One day, two of the directors from E.K Construction arrived to tell Carl and his co-director, Sam Donovan, that the group was in serious trouble because of some difficulties with commercial contracts, and that they would be closing all the regional offices, including Exeter. They said that the company could not afford to pay redundancy, but that they could buy the practice. Carl was irate, since he had been largely responsible for building it and now it was in trouble because of the commercial contracts that E.K Construction had forced them to undertake. He was happy as an employee, but now he would be forced to become self-employed – with all the risk that involved – at a time when, with three lots of school fees, a large mortgage, and a wife who did not want to work, he needed to minimize his financial risk.

Carl and Sam bought the practice for a token amount, since they were effectively buying £25,000 worth of debt. Carl was not enthusiastic about becoming a co-owner of the business with Sam, but he had no choice. Sam was not a chartered engineer, and not particularly dedicated to his job. Carl had opposed his promotion, but Sam had done a good job of ingratiating himself with the E.K. Construction directors, and they called the shots.

Things then became very difficult for Carl. Two of the major commercial projects went wrong, and neither client would pay. Sam and he argued constantly about money, and while Carl was working all hours, it seemed to him that Sam put in no extra effort at all and, as Sam was not chartered, he had to rely very heavily on Carl.

It was therefore a relief when Sam announced that he wanted out. His departure required some legal disentangling and, unsurprisingly, Sam did not want to pay off his share of the debt. After some heated exchanges, Carl decided to let him go without paying: 'I suppose it was naïve of me, and he certainly had a better lawyer than I did, but really I didn't have any appetite for the fight. I'd had enough of him and I just didn't have any energy left – the business was taking all I'd got.'

At least Carl was his own boss, but he was now facing a cash flow crisis and so he went to the bank. The bank was very supportive, but required him to remortgage his house as security for the loan he needed, and he also had to use his pension fund to support his finances. This left the business in a viable financial position, but Carl was far deeper in debt. He could not talk to his wife about it; she was not interested in the business, never had been. She always presumed, in what to him was an alarming way, that he would earn the money somehow.

Carl struggled on for a short while, but the commercial contracts were a huge drain on his time, preventing him from winning more of the public sector business that was his strength. He watched the bank interest piling up, and realized that he would have to do something to change the balance of his finances. The hardest part was telling his wife that they would have to move from their lovely new house to something much smaller. She did not take it well – in fact she refused to move. This only added to all the stress he was under and, for a time, he considered giving it all up, but then he did win a good contract and his wife came round to the idea of moving. He had given her an ultimatum – either we move or the children go to state schools. She agreed, and they moved to a much smaller house in a much cheaper area. This lifted the burden considerably because they were able to pay off the mortgage and some of the company debt too. Nonetheless, it took four years to recover the situation completely and, although this was partly due to all the inherited problems, Carl did add to his troubles in two ways:

'I decided to manage with the minimum number of staff – two junior engineers and a part-time administrator. Unfortunately, I made a couple of disastrous selection decisions, which cost me time, money and, worst of all, reputation. One recruit was a bright young graduate engineer, with wonderful interpersonal skills. She had no trouble selling herself to me and to my clients, but sadly she did not deliver technically, and her attention to detail, so vital in engineering, was poor. I kept giving her second chances which led to some embarrassing situations in front of clients, but then one of these situations eventually ended up in court, with a serious financial dispute, and only then did I do what I should have done at the beginning, and fired her.

'I suppose I overreacted then, and brought in a chap who had excellent credentials and references but who, unlike his predecessor, was very quiet and unassuming. I lost on both counts with him. He was indeed very quiet and studious and tried very hard, but he really wasn't anywhere near as good as his references suggested. He lacked confidence in his abilities, which I was soon to discover was an accurate assessment on his part. Although I struggled to make something of him, he really did not progress and, after six wasted months, I asked him to leave.

'During this time, another of my commercial client relationships had gone sour, and indeed he turned out to be a professional con man in the property game. I said goodbye to our fees on that job, knowing that if it came to a battle of lawyers, he would almost certainly win. I've learned the bitter lesson of checking out new clients before undertaking any major work for them.

'I also learned the lesson about my terrible recruitment decisions. I actually paid a small fee to a friend, Adriana, who works in HR for a big pharmaceutical company to come and help me recruit my engineers. I was expecting some intuitive assessment, but far from it, she was very practical and systematic in her approach – all common sense when you think about it. She suggested that they did practical tests so that I could actually see them working and, with input from me, she devised lots of "How would you deal with this situation or problem?" type questions, which we asked every candidate. She arranged for them to have some informal waiting time chatting to Tina, my administrator, and asked her opinion too. At assessment time, she had a simple rule: "If in doubt, cross them out!" When it came to references, Adriana rang the referees up, and had some clever questions like, 'Did XXX change and

develop over the time they worked for you? If so, in what way?'
By this time, though, references were just a formality because
we'd put them through the mill and were pretty confident about
our decision, and so it proved. I couldn't be more pleased with
the result.

'Now I'm out of the commercial markeplace, and back on my
home ground in the public sector with a nice portfolio of clients,
two excellent junior engineers, no debt, and a good reputation.'

Lessons learned

Carl was frank with Helen, the company doctor, about a
fundamental issue.

'I suppose I have to ask myself whether I really wanted my own
business. I was catapulted into it by events and I felt huge
ownership of my practice, which I'd helped to build up but,
really, I should have thought harder about what I wanted before
I got dragged down what has been a long and painful road. I
was happy as an employee, and would have stayed that way if
the company hadn't gone bust. Of course I wouldn't go back
now but, looking at what I went through and the stress it put on
me and my marriage and family, I'm not really sure it was worth
it. I didn't stand back and make a proper decision – I just fell
into it.

'What I should have done and didn't, and this is a fault
throughout, is to talk it through with someone independent,
with no axe to grind. I have an old school friend who's a civil
servant. Great bloke and a good listener, but he doesn't really
have a clue what I do, and so I didn't feel able to discuss things
with him fully. Since I asked Adriana to help me with the
recruitment, I've talked a few things through with her and that's
been enormously helpful. I should have found more 'Adrianas'
from the start, and taken their advice, or at least used them as
sounding boards.

'I should also have networked more, and found out who the
movers and shakers were in the areas in which I was working.
That con man had quite a reputation, and if I'd had my ear to
the ground, I would have found that out. I was too preoccupied
with my own problems, too internally focused. A few beers and
lunches might have seemed frivolous at the time, but they would
have saved me a lot of money and heartache.

'I've invested too much time in lost causes, like my staff. I've learned that it's easier to face up to a problem early, as the longer you leave it, the harder it gets. If someone isn't performing, then set standards and give them help, but if you don't get a good response, cut your losses. It's easier for everyone in the long run.

'I should also have been tougher with Sam. I should not have allowed him to escape without paying his share of the debts. I just wanted him to go, and couldn't face the hassle, but really if I'd spelled it out clearly to him as soon as he raised the subject of leaving, I would have got a better result – maybe not everything, but certainly more than I did get, which was nothing! What I didn't do was to think through fully the effects of the debt burden. If I'd done that, with just a few figures, I would have seen what a mess I was heading for, and made Sam pay. As it was, I just had this feeling that he was more of a hindrance than a help, and I'd do better on my own, which wasn't strictly true.

'I suppose I treated my wife too gently too. I should have been much clearer with her. I tried to protect her from our financial reality for too long, which put a huge amount of stress on me. I should have spelled it out from the beginning, presented her with the facts, and asked her what action she thought we should take. Instead, I said little for ages, then told her we had to move to a smaller house. It's not surprising she said no. If she'd known the facts early on, she'd have reached the inevitable conclusion long before I worked up the courage to tell her.'

Success tactics

Here is a summary of Helen's conclusions (the company doctor), which fall under the following headings:

- Plan and evaluate
- Getting and taking advice
- Good business relationships
- Getting the best from your people
- Ability to balance home and work.

Plan and evaluate

'When the unexpected strikes, it is very tempting to plunge in and get busy, but it is vital to think before you react. Carl needed a realistic projection of where the business was going financially, including all the high-risk projects. An assessment of the job market would also have been wise. Armed with all this information, he could have made a decision about whether or not to take on the business, and what he needed from Sam. Without this data he was swept along, hoping for the best, and getting the worst.'

Getting and taking advice

'For Carl, as for many people, it becomes obvious that you needed advice after the event, when you have failed to take it. He should have sought financial, legal and personnel advice, and could have done with some personal advice too about managing his wife, and about being employed or self-employed. He needed, and still does not have, a business buddy.'

Good business relationships

'Carl had a network of contacts, but they were not in the commercial sector. He did not like the commercial sector, but he was stuck with it, and therefore he should have got to know people in that area. It would not have taken him long to find out about the con man, had he done this.'

Getting the best from your people

'I have to question whether a different Carl would have made something of Sam, and avoided the schism. This may or may not be the case as I cannot judge without spending some time with Sam. As far as the disastrous hires were concerned, Carl appears to have genuinely tried with them, but clearly it took him a long time to recognize a sow's ear, and he spent too long on both of them. Now he has two motivated and effective engineers, which suggests that his problem is all about selection, and not about managing people well.'

Ability to balance home and work

'Carl made the classic mistake of trying to protect his wife from the problems he was facing. There may also have been an element of self-protection too – not wanting her to know how things had gone from bad to worse since he took over the business. Whatever the reasons, he ended up under double stress: bearing the burden himself, and then finding that she did not accept his solution.

'If you have a partner who is not interested or is unsupportive, a buddy is vital to enable you to share your worries with someone, to discuss how to manage your home life and whether you want to be an employee or to run your own business.'

Your health check

Key questions to ask:

1 Is this business what I really want?
2 Do I have someone I can confide in about the business?
3 Does my network of contacts provide me with useful data?
4 How do I ensure that I hire and train only silk purses?
5 How easy is it for me to ask for advice?
6 How well do I plan for the future?

part 2

solutions: the top tactics for success

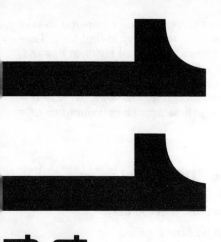

the key—
finding time

In this chapter you will learn:
- how to recognize the signs
- how to work out what is important
- to make the changes stick
- delegation
- about the too-difficult pile
- about finding help and support.

We begin Part 2 with a success tactic that will equip you to take on all the other tactics that follow: the ability to find time. Time is often the most precious commodity a small business has and, by reading this chapter, you will find enough of it to be able to apply what you learn, and make those success tactics work for you. If you start to feel uncomfortable, and want to skip this chapter or dismiss its content, these are classic symptoms of a time victim, so read on!

How to recognize the signs

The surest sign that you are not managing your time well is if you are saying the famous words, 'I'm too busy.'

- Too busy just doing, with no time for thinking.
- Too busy to spend time with friends or family.
- Too busy to get some advice about a problem that keeps nagging at the back of your mind.

Thinking is probably the most important thing that people who run small businesses do not find time for. There is so much to do, and doing is so much easier than thinking! Overwork gives you the perfect excuse, and only when something forces you to take stock, such as a bad debt, do you start thinking, by which time it may be too late.

As a result of not thinking, you will probably not find the time to get support or advice – to find people who might help you to see that you are not operating effectively.

Although you are not thinking much, you do still register problems. You may end up with a list of things to worry about, but you do not find time to address them so they just sit there, sapping your energy as you worry about them.

Because you are so busy, you do not have time for yourself. Time to check how you are feeling in general, and whether your passion, focus and commitment to the business are as strong as ever. There is a proven link between stress and health and, if you are sitting on a pile of worries at the same time as you are overworking, the chances are that your body will decide you need a rest, even if you do not, and you will end up with colds, flu or worse.

You may also have little or no time for family or friends. You may find that this creates friction, and may lead to a breakdown in a relationship. This then makes your worry pile even bigger.

Sadly, most of us know of businesses that have gone bust, with the owner suffering in health and their marriage in ruins.

Working out what is important

Having painted these bleak pictures, you may be wondering how to find the time to avoid all these problems. Start by reading the following story. You may have encountered it before, but it illustrates beautifully how to approach this challenge.

One day, an expert in time management was speaking to a group of business students and, to drive home a point, he used an illustration those students have never forgotten. As he stood in front of the group of high-powered overachievers, he said, 'Okay, time for a quiz.' Then he pulled out a 4.5-litre wide-mouthed jar and set it on the table in front of him. Next he produced about a dozen fist-sized rocks and carefully placed them, one at a time, into the jar.

When the jar was filled to the top and no more rocks would fit inside, he asked, 'Is this jar full?' Everyone in the class said, 'Yes'. Then he said, 'Really?' He reached under the table and pulled out a bucket of gravel. Then he dumped some gravel in and shook the jar, causing pieces of gravel to work themselves down into the space between the big rocks. Then he asked the group once more, 'Is the jar full?' By this time the class was on to him. 'Probably not,' one of them answered.

'Good!' he replied. He reached under the table and brought out a bucket of sand. He started dumping the sand in the jar, and it went into all of the spaces left between the rocks and the gravel.

Once more he asked the question, 'Is this jar full?' 'No!' The class shouted. Once again he said, 'Good.' Then he grabbed a pitcher of water and began to pour it in until the jar was filled to the brim.

Then he looked at the class and asked, 'What is the point of this illustration?' One eager beaver raised his hand and said, 'The point is, no matter how full your schedule is, if you try really hard you can always fit some more things in it!' 'No,' the speaker replied, 'That's not the point. The truth this illustration teaches us is: if you don't put the big rocks in first, you'll never get them in at all.'

What are the 'big rocks' in your business and your life? Monitoring and evaluating your business is a big rock. Just running your business could be gravel, sand or water.

Your health, your friends, your family – these are also big rocks. And what about your personal development, your hobbies, a worthy cause, doing things that you love, time for yourself? These could also be your big rocks and, if you do not put them in the jar first, they are guaranteed not to fit once you get busy on all that gravel and sand, not to mention the water. You can fill your working life with all the day-to-day duties of operating your business, but never have the quality time to spend on what is really important and, in business terms, as a minimum that means evaluating and planning.

You may hold the belief that you can fit in a planning or a family rock later, 'When things have calmed down a bit' or 'When I have a free weekend'. This is more of the same 'too busy' syndrome. How do you know that there will be a 'later'? How do you know that it will not be too late?

Is there anything stopping you from planning how to spend your life? Most likely this exercise will force you to face up to some difficult home truths, and you may not like the thought of that, but that is all the more reason to do it. So, look at your big rocks, and check that you have put them all in the jar. If some are still lying outside, ask why. What beliefs do you hold about them that mean they don't fit? Maybe some of the big rocks in the jar should be pebbles. Lay them all out and decide how you want to spend your work and your personal life.

Here is a checklist of rocks which you may wish to include:

1 Your family.
2 Your health.
3 Your work.
4 Your friends.
5 Your hobbies.
6 Your personal development.
7 Your dreams.
8 Time to yourself .

This stage is quite important, so give yourself time! Whatever feels wrong, whatever does not fit, take time to work out why. Some of the rocks may carry a 'too difficult' label and you may be tempted to leave them out of your jar because of that. You will know, by the feelings of conflict that stem from this, that the rock should be in the jar. Health might be an example – you know you do not exercise, you eat badly and you do not get enough sleep – but you dismiss this as a temporary problem, and not a rock, except that it keeps nagging at you. This is a clear sign that you need to include it as a rock.

Making it happen

When you have put the rocks in the jar, you may think that you have a pile of sand and gravel that will not fit. Do not worry about this, otherwise you will end up back where you started; just plan to give the big rocks priority, and build a schedule to include them. Often you will find that the sand and gravel still fit because you deal with them more efficiently, or someone else does, or you discover that you do not need to do them so often or even at all. You may be surprised at what a major readjustment of priorities can produce.

Making the changes stick

When you are happy with your rocks, the next stage is to work out how you will keep them in the jar. Again, this is a matter of beliefs. If time with your children is a rock but you always work late and never see them, ask yourself what belief is driving your behaviour. Could it be a belief based on the old work ethic, telling you that work is valuable and worthy, whereas 'play' with the kids is not? It is easy to reframe this belief: if you are playing with the kids, you are doing your duty as a parent. For some people, parental duty is just as important as working hard, and so they are able to leave work on time to do their parental duty.

Another way to reframe the belief is to relate it to time and opportunity. Listen to the many parents who say that they wished they had spent more time with their children. Do you ever hear people say that they wished they had spent more time in the office? Your time with your children is short, and children change every day. You cannot save them up for later, they will have left home by then.

To increase your commitment to the new set of priorities that your rocks represent, you could discuss them with your partner, spouse or the person they involve. You may find that what you think is important to them is not their first priority, and they may have alternative suggestions. They may also help you to find other ways of meeting your goals. Just the fact that you have told someone else about your new priorities will also increase your own commitment to these priorities.

The business jar

When you first do the rocks in the jar exercise, it is vital to do it in the context of your whole life. When you know how big your work/business rock is, you may find it helpful at a later stage to have a business-only jar, where you apply exactly the same principles to determine your business priorities and, in particular, to prioritize what is important, such as finding a new market, against what is urgent, such as filling in your tax return. The first is a rock, but the second is gravel disguised as a rock! The amount of 'non-work' rocks may have made your overall business jar smaller, that is, you have less time for work due to personal and home life activities. Therefore, you may need to be more ruthless in how you prioritize your work time, and find other resources to handle the things that you do not need to deal with personally.

Delegation

If you have people working for you, they may surprise you by handling bigger pieces of gravel – or even rocks – than you have previously thought them capable of. One of the biggest time stealers is an unwillingness to delegate. If you recognize this as a problem, then examine your beliefs about delegation. Here are some examples that might match your thinking:

- Nobody else does it as well as I do.
- I want to be sure it's done the right way.
- They can't really cope with this.
- They might make a mess of it.
- It's quicker to do it myself.

If any of these rings a bell, they are the classic beliefs of people who are unwilling to delegate. They believe that other people are not as competent, able to learn or as trustworthy as they are. Usually they will have carefully proven this theory by throwing a poor soul in at the deep end with little or no training or guidance, and then, having watched them fail, they will sadly announce, 'I knew they'd make a mess of it. It's quicker to do it myself in future.'

If you recognize yourself in any of this, start by addressing your beliefs about your staff, because if you do not, you will just be proved right again. If you can allow yourself to believe that Susie might be able to help with the books, given some training, then Susie stands a chance of doing so. Now you have a responsibility to train her well, not just throw a few instructions at her and leave her to it – you want her to succeed, remember?

If you are still not quite sure that you do want her to succeed, address those feelings of insecurity, because that is what they are. By ensuring that only you can do certain things, you are reinforcing your superiority – often quite unconsciously. Why do you need to compete with your own staff, you might want to ask yourself? Think, instead, that what they become is down to you. You can take the credit for a skilled and effective team, rather than taking the credit for doing the work yourself.

Of course, you really like doing the work yourself, that is also part of the problem. However, some of these big rocks will take you out of your comfort zone, and you will look for excuses to slip back into it. Determine to get comfortable with these rocks, either by yourself, or through getting help. You may have to grit your teeth a little at the beginning, but then you will find huge satisfaction when you do get to grips with them.

The too-difficult pile

Where you see a 'too difficult' label appearing on a rock, tackle it head on, using a 'ten-minute' approach. For example, cash flow may look like a big rock, and you fear that inventory may be the root of the problem. You know you have far too much of it, but you like to stock a wide range, and your suppliers' deliveries are erratic. You can see that you have a lot of money tied up in there, but it is going to be a big job to sort it out and you just do not have the energy, never mind the time.

This is a classic example of something from which we all suffer: things that we ought to do that we do not get around to doing. If you examine the reasons for this, they tend to fall into three major areas:

1 Can do it, but I dislike doing it.
2 Can't face it.
3 Very hard – need help.

As a technique, start by giving yourself just ten minutes to look at the issue. After ten minutes, you can put it back on the pile and go back to your 'normal' role. Use those ten minutes to work out what this rock involves. Just make a list of what you think needs doing. If you do not know, then it is a category 3 problem (see previous page).

Book another ten minutes to revisit the list. If you do not have a list because the issue is in category 3, make a list of where to get help or even who to ask to find out where to get help. The objective of these ten-minute sessions is to help you to break down a task into its components so that you discover one of three things:

1 First, that you can do it after all and, once you start, it is really not that bad. This is of course the best outcome, which you have reached by having one or two short planning sessions to clarify exactly what needs to be done.

2 Second, you discover that you can do it, that it has to be you who does it, and you really do not want to do it. As an example of how to deal with this, suppose that your rock is clearly labelled 'selling'. You are a consultant, and you are coming to the end of a big project and you do not have a pipeline of prospective clients. You know you need to sell, but you do not like selling, so you put it off. You hope that the project will be extended, but secretly you know that this will not happen. Start by examining your beliefs about selling:

• You may believe that you are no good at it.

• You may think that people hate receiving sales calls, so that means they are going to hate you.

• You may believe that it is a rather unsavoury activity, unnecessary if you were to win business the 'proper' way, through referrals.

With any of these beliefs, it is hardly surprising to find that the 'selling' rock is not sitting happily in the jar. To get it in there, work on some of those beliefs. If changing them is too big a stretch, then take them on temporarily, just while you are selling.

For example, you are a consultant – you help people. You are not selling, you are offering help – you are good at that. Your prospect might not need your help, so never mind, maybe another time. This is a very different way of thinking from the 'foot in the door' sales image which you may carry in your head.

If you still struggle with selling, find other ways to win clients: by networking or by becoming an associate of a company who does the selling for you. Now you may find your 'selling' rock has disappeared and been replaced by a smaller one called 'find a company that needs associates like me'.

Another reason why you may be so reluctant to do something might involve a difficult personal interchange – disciplining one of your team, for example – which you keep putting off. Naturally, the more you put it off, the harder it gets. You may know exactly what to do, you know that only you can do it, so what may help here is a rehearsal with a sympathetic listener who can give you feedback and enable you to feel much more prepared and therefore resourceful when you do the real thing.

3 Third, you discover that you really do need help or you need to find someone else to do it, and your task then becomes finding the best source of assistance.

Finding help and support

Think of support in its broadest sense – a chat with your partner over lunch at the weekend might be helpful, even if they know little about the business. At the other end of the spectrum, if you know you need more funding and do not have a clue where to start, think of it first as an exercise in selecting advisers.

Advice does not always mean an expensive consultant, so do not dismiss it with 'can't afford it'. Even if it is expensive, it can be money well spent, with huge savings in the long run, so do not use cost as a reason to struggle on alone. 'Can't afford it' is a plea to be treated with suspicion as it tends to follow closely on the heels of 'I'm too busy' in the list of reasons not to do things in small businesses. Ask yourself 'Can I afford not to?' as a starting point, and think of the return you might get on this investment.

Buddy

An excellent way of getting support and advice is to find a business buddy. This is someone who can speak your business language without necessarily being an expert or without operating in the same area. The basis of the relationship is that you help each other. One of you may want to talk through the decision to hire more staff; the other may be unsure about buying premises and want to discuss the pros and cons.

This is a particularly helpful relationship, especially when you do not have anyone else in the business to discuss things with, and it is worth doing some networking or research to identify a buddy, although you may already know someone who fits the bill. Their role is much more of a sounding board than a source of information, and together you can create the space for the thinking and planning which you might not manage on your own.

Balance

Time spent on your business does not always equate to an improved business result. Of course, you need serious dedication to the business, but if you can build in a level of balance, be it time with your family, on your boat, or wherever you want to be, you are likely to deliver more effectively as a result. This applies even if you hold Noel Coward's view that 'work is more fun than fun!' You will still benefit from a break from work. The less fun work is, the more breaks you need. If work is no fun at all, then it is time to take stock and turn to Chapter 15, 'A passion for what you do'.

If you have felt uncomfortable reading this chapter, and feel inclined to dismiss it or to 'think about it later', recognize that you are showing the classic symptoms it describes, and give it time now. We tend to think of time management as a minor issue but, in the context of our whole life, nothing is more important.

Steps to success

Key questions to ask:

1 Am I happy with how I spend my time at work and outside it?
2 Can I fit all my priorities, including work, into my jar?
3 If not, what is stopping me?
   a My beliefs
   b My inability to delegate
   c My 'too-difficult' pile
4 Do I need help?
5 Can I make the changes stick?
6 Can I do all this now?
7 If can't do it all now, what is more important to me than planning how to spend my life?

12

to lead or to manage the business?

In this chapter you will learn:
- the differences between leadership and management
- about delegated and DIY management
- about planning, administration and execution.

Managing is one of those words that can mean everything and nothing. Obviously, I manage the business, you may be thinking, but perhaps you are better suited to leading the business than managing it. Maybe you have not thought that there is a distinction between the two.

The difference between leadership and management

Leading means having the vision, the passion and the drive to take your business forward. You may be a brilliant chemist with a new cosmetic idea that you can promote to your contacts in the business. You can create the formula yourself, and have a brilliant touch when it comes to balancing ingredients. This is all part of creating your vision and setting the company direction.

Managing, on the other hand, is about making things happen efficiently. It is composed of three key elements, none of which is leadership. They are planning, administration, execution and, if there are staff involved, getting the best out of people. These three skills are not related, and someone who is good with people may be useless at planning. Equally, a good administrator is not necessarily a planner or a people person.

When you start out in business, you tend to be a jack-of-all-trades, then as the business develops, your role begins to change. As you grow, you need more administration and planning, neither of which may be your forte, but because this happens gradually you may not think about it until a problem forces you to take stock.

Our creative chemist may think up lots of new lines for her product range, but she may not think much about the company's cash position. Her planning skills need to extend to all areas of the business, yet she may not be very interested in figures. She may hold the belief that if she just keeps inventing and selling more lines, success must follow. With that view she may be heading for the graveyard of so many successful businesses that ran out of cash with a full and profitable order book.

The aim of this chapter is to provide an analysis of exactly what management a business needs, and then to enable you to map your skills and preferences on to that analysis, to find the gaps or problems, and to address them. There are specific chapters on managing your time (Chapter 11), your finances (Chapter 13), your people (Chapter 18) and on business planning (Chapter 14). This chapter looks at management in general, and serves as an introduction to the areas covered in the other chapters.

Leadership

You are unlikely to have started a business without some elements of leadership. You had the vision and knew what you wanted to achieve. It is vital to recognize that you can be a leader without also being a manager – other people can do that, and it does not mean that you are relinquishing some essential function that only you can perform. You must lead, as the owner of a small business, but you do not have to manage.

Delegated management

You may think that you do not have the luxury of being able to get someone else to do your managing for you, so you are going to have to do it yourself. Check this thinking before you continue because managers are not necessarily expensive, senior people. They may come surprisingly cheap, and you may be able to spend your own time far more usefully and profitably if you hand over management to someone else.

Case study

Betsy is married, in her early fifties and her children have left home. She works three days a week, handling administration, doing your financial forecasts and keeping an eye on the sales office. She is a good 'manager', and she is not expensive. This does not mean that you are exploiting her – simply that the role you have given her is not a complete, stand-alone management position; it includes a good deal of basic administration. You pay her fairly at a rate which is high for an administrator, and low for a supervisor. She is very happy – she likes the job, the people, the hours and the location. You are happy because you are getting a great contribution from her, and you are able to use your time so much better.

DIY management

If you have done the numbers and you cannot justify even a Betsy, you will have to continue (or possibly start) doing it yourself. Begin by deciding exactly what it is that you have to do using the following analysis.

People management

If you employ staff, they need managing. This is dealt with in Chapter 18, and here we will say no more on this topic, except the caveat that any employee needs active managing. Do not ignore old Jack, your only employee, who comes in twice a week to do the packing – he needs managing too; as do any self-employed people who work for you or contractors, such as a distribution service, that deliver for you every week.

Planning – taking control

Planning is covered in Chapter 14, but here we want to look at it in the broadest business context. What do we mean, exactly when we say planning? Planning covers the following:

- Your market(s)
- Your products/services
- Your finances – profit and cash
- Your staffing/premises/equipment
- Your suppliers
- Yourself.

Planning might mean having a written plan, but more often it will mean having a plan in your head which gives you a clear idea of where you are heading in each area.

The critical point is that you are in control of all aspects of the business. You have thought about how they are running and either you are happy to let them continue, or they need some attention. You review operations regularly – perhaps monthly, perhaps quarterly, never less frequently than that. The key is to anticipate problems, not wait for them to push you into action.

'If it ain't broke, don't fix it' can be a good motto, but it does not allow for the fact that something might be in the process of breaking. So, when that supplier whose deliveries had become erratic finally goes bust, that is not the time to start researching a source of supply for your most critical component. Your supplier plan should ensure that you always have a back-up source, so there will be no scrabbling about and getting a poor deal because you are desperate. And neither will there be any delays to supplying your customers.

The supplier plan referred to here is not a fancy document. It is a list of all your key suppliers, with details of a secondary source beside each one. You check these secondary sources at least once a year – to make sure they are still in business – and perhaps you might order from them too. How you do this is up to you. The point is that you are proactively managing your supplier base, not just in case of a failure, but also to keep your eye on prices and on what is available in the market. This will keep your current suppliers on their toes too – not by any threats on your part, but just by knowing that you have a policy of back-up suppliers and of keeping your eye on their marketplace.

Planning and evaluation means that you look at each area of your business, on a regular basis, and ask the following questions:

- Is it working well?
- Could it work better/cheaper/faster?
- What could go wrong?
- What would I do if it did go wrong?

Planning will ensure that you keep your business under review and that you are constantly looking for ways to improve and to take steps to avert any crises well before they occur. You yourself are on the list of things to plan because you are central to the way the business runs. If you are not working well, then it is just as critical to face your own difficulties as it is to face those of your suppliers or your staff. Your problem might be overwork, or loss of focus, or health. As long as you face it square on, and do not try to carry on regardless, you will find a solution before a problem becomes a crisis.

Administration and execution

Administration is a word that seems to mean everything and nothing. It conjures up images of bureaucrats filling in endless forms, and has a generally low-level, boring connotation. In fact, execution would be a better word, not only because it has more dramatic connotations than administration, but because it is about getting things done. Administration is the invisible oil that feeds all the components of an operation, and results in real efficiency.

Administration also covers VAT returns and ordering stationery, but the big piece is the link between all parts of your operation. You may have computer systems that cover every aspect of what you do, but they will not make things happen by themselves. Whether you have comprehensive IT (information technology) systems or not, you will need good business processes, and some personal oil applied to them too.

When there is only one of you, for example, Sally who makes pottery dolls, you work it out as you go along: Sally works out the best mix of dolls for processing together, the packaging materials to use and the delivery method. When she gets in her two temporary helpers for big orders, Sally needs to formalize the process to explain it to them. Orders for Ireland go in those special green boxes, and the client has requested extra packaging. The invoice must go on the outside of the box, not inside – whereas her customer in Wales wants the invoices sent separately.

One way of looking at administration would be to add it to your list of items under planning and evaluation, addressing questions like:

- Are we using the most efficient methods in processing orders from enquiry to delivery?
- Are we efficient in the way we handle all our documentation and financial transactions, including VAT?
- Are we consistently successful in winning new business?

If you have staff doing any of these things, involve them in the review. They do the work, so they see the problems first hand. This discussion itself will be part of your lubricating oil, because your staff are analysing together how to work more effectively, which is the focus you want them to have. They may realize that there are communication gaps they need to fill, or steps that are duplicated, or which can be omitted. You can sit and watch because the discussion may well take off without you. Ensure at the end that actions are recorded and that all actions have an owner – preferably not you – and then arrange a review meeting to see how the changes are progressing. This is lubrication oil that you are pouring on to an increasingly efficient operation.

If you have no staff, and have to deal with administration yourself, the same questions apply, and you can ask yourself if you are operating as efficiently as you might be. You could also ask a business buddy and, if you are considering a serious investment in new software for the business, it may be worth investing in some professional advice to make sure that you buy the right accounting package, for example. Part of good management is knowing when you need advice, and not being afraid to ask.

If you have to do all the administration yourself, it would be as well to list it all, and then use the list as a checklist – say, every month – to be sure that nothing has slipped through. You may be immensely well organized, in which case ignore these comments: but you may also be the kind of person who forgets to raise invoices now and again, in which case you need every kind of reminder. Chapter 14 gives more detail on the methods you can use to ensure that good administrative habits stick. The secret is to find a good reason to do these things, and this will either be because you know they are important and value them, or because you like doing them.

Case studies

Sarah finds numbers very boring, but likes charts, and enjoys playing with spreadsheet software packages. All of her business data is now in chart form – whenever she updates any figures, she immediately sees the results in a graph, bar or pie chart, which she finds very satisfying, and it serves to give her an excellent financial feel for her business.

Joe, on the other hand, dislikes paperwork and 'screen' work of any kind, but he has just had a nasty shock when he realized that he was about to go overdrawn at the bank. A cheque he paid in has not cleared, and he has a pile of invoices to send out. He resolves to invoice immediately, or within two days maximum in future, and finds a red file to sit on his desk with the order details ready to be processed. He also puts a reminder sticker on his PC. He will not notice it after a while, but he hopes by then to have got into good habits. He still hates doing it, but now he sees the point – he had never sailed so close to the wind before.

In summary, when you ask yourself the question 'Am I managing the business well?', break it down immediately into its three component parts:

1 Planning
2 Administration and execution
3 People

Thinking of management in these three areas makes it much easier to focus on. As with everything else in the business, the message is to grab it by the throat (not literally, in the case of your staff), and make sure that you are in control of it. Then, when you are happy, you can let it run for a time until the next review point. This is proactive management of the business to make sure that you are running it, and that it is not running you.

Steps to success

Key questions to ask:

1 Do I want to lead or manage the business, or both?
2 Do I enjoy managing? If not, who else could do it?
3 How well and how often do I plan?
4 How well do I handle the administration?
5 How smooth and efficient is my operation?
6 If I have staff, do I get the best from them?
7 Do I need help – from a buddy, a colleague, or a professional?
8 If I do need help, where can I get it from?

13

a financial feel for the business

In this chapter you will learn:
- to understand profit
- to understand cash
- the differences between cash and profit
- how to manage your cash flow
- how to manage your profit.

Developing a financial feel for the business is not about becoming an accountant, nor about doing complex calculations. It is about developing a simple understanding of the way your business works financially so that you cultivate an ability to recognize a pattern in what you do, and are therefore able to detect any changes in that pattern before serious problems arise.

Just common sense, you may think, which it is but, since running out of cash is the cause of over 80 per cent of small business failures, then it is obviously not that common! There are two models to consider – the first is about profit, the second is about cash – and it is the confusion of these two which lies at the root of many catastrophes. We shall use the example of Sally, who makes pottery dolls, to illustrate thse models.

Understanding profit

Figure 1 shows the structure of Sally's business. She makes pottery dolls in her garden shed, which also serves as a shop. She supplies some dolls by mail order, and advertises monthly in *Doll Collector's Gazette*.

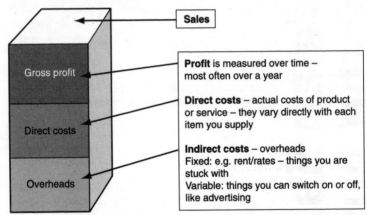

Figure 1 Structure of Sally's business

When you deduct direct costs and overheads from Sally's sales figure, her gross profit is what she has left.

Costs and profit

The direct costs vary with each doll she makes – clay, glaze, postage and packing materials all fall into this category.

The overheads are indirect costs, and they fall into two groups:

1 Fixed overheads are costs that Sally incurs anyway, whether she makes one doll or 50. Heating and rent would be examples of these. As she owns the house, Sally simply charges a set proportion of the costs of running it to the business.

2 Variable overheads are general costs that Sally can choose to spend, and which are not directly related to what she makes. Advertising is a good example – she can switch it on or off, irrespective of how many dolls she produces.

When Sally adds all these direct and indirect costs together, and deducts them from her selling price for the number of dolls she has sold in the period, she gets her gross profit figure. From this will be deducted any interest charges on money borrowed (none, in Sally's case), and tax she pays on the business; then what is left is all hers – her net profit after tax.

Sally describes her feel for the business:

'I want to keep my costs really low, and my prices high – that makes me comfortable because I cannot predict volume yet. My fixed costs are negligible, so that if I didn't sell a single doll it would not matter. I have some money in trust which pays all the bills and gives me just enough to live on, so I do not rely on the business to feed me.

'I'm tempted to buy clay in bulk, but I've nowhere to put it, and it ties up a lot of cash, so I pay more for smaller deliveries. I am hoping to negotiate better terms for regular orders when I have a good track record established.'

Understanding cash

What would Sally do if she suddenly received a huge and very profitable order? To make that decision, she needs to consider her cash position. This works on a different time frame from profit – cash is the business of today, of the moment, what you have now, whereas profit is measured over a set period of a month or a year.

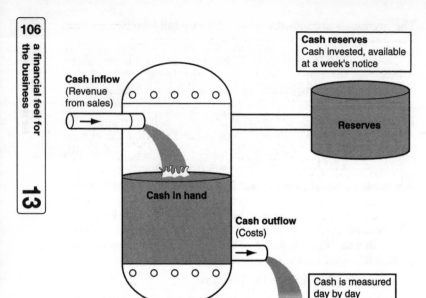

Cash reserves
Cash invested, available
at a week's notice

Cash inflow
(Revenue
from sales)

Reserves

Cash in hand

Cash outflow
(Costs)

Cash is measured
day by day

Figure 2 Cash flow

Cash is simply what you have in the bank, plus what money comes in on the day, less the bills you have to pay today. Think of cash as being the air your business breathes. Your business can be fit, healthy and very profitable, but deprive it of air for the briefest time and you kill your business, no matter how healthy (profitable) it was.

In Figure 2, air is depicted (so that you can see it!) as a flowing liquid. Money feeds into the business, and while it flows to feed cash going out, all is well. If the cash runs out and the air no longer flows, your business will not survive.

The difference between cash and profit

If you think of the analogy of air and cash in Figure 2, it will clarify the general confusion between cash and profit. If Sally were to take that big order for dolls, it would look great as far as profit goes, but if she gets paid 30 days after delivery, how is she going to pay for all the clay, the extra help, the packing materials and so on?

The obvious answer is that she will not pay her suppliers until she herself has been paid, but suppose her client does not pay in 30 days, suppose they take 90 days, as some big companies do? If she can also take 90 days that might work, but she knows the clay supplier would not settle for that, and her temp would not wait three months for his pay. Here is the essence of the confusion: a piece of good, highly profitable business could make her bankrupt because she does not have the cash to fund it. This is one of the classic mistakes made in business, and it happens over and over again (see Figure 3). People say yes to a profitable deal, without realizing the cash implications 'because profitable business must be good, mustn't it?'

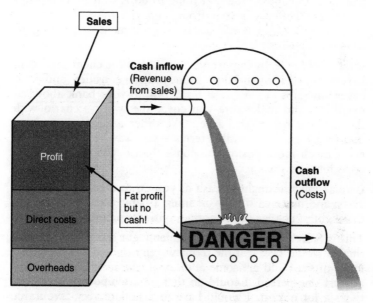

Figure 3 Profit vs cash

There are two other contributing factors to exacerbate this problem. Optimism is the first – the belief that it will be all right on the night – because this is such good business, we can't go wrong, and they'll pay up because they'll be so delighted. Always assume that large organizations are bad payers and will take at least 90 days, which will be a good place to start your calculations.

The second contributing factor is that you are probably quite prompt in paying your bills. As a small business you need to be, otherwise suppliers can refuse to deal with you. The opposite is usually true of large organisations, who know exactly what they can get away with. As a one-off, you may be able to negotiate extended terms with your suppliers, but it is something that would not be easily repeated, so it should only be done in the direst of circumstances. The obvious conclusion is that you will have paid all your bills by the time your client gets around to paying you. If you really want to play safe with cash, you could make a contingency plan assuming that the supplier did not pay you at all. Now you are really thinking hard about cash flow planning. Obviously, the best thing to do is to negotiate better terms. Try 100 per cent upfront, and you may find you get 50 per cent, which is still a vast improvement on waiting 90 days for the whole lot!

If the order is really important to you, and the client solid gold in terms of their financial position, you can consider funding to cover any gaps in your cash flow. Talk to your bank about an overdraft, and make sure you cover the worst scenario with them. Do it before you accept the order and after you have negotiated the best possible terms – this way you are likely to get a much more positive response than if you wait until the crisis hits and then ask.

Give as much thought to cash as you do to profit or clients or costs, and make cash flow planning a habit when there is even the slightest change in the normal business pattern.

This is Sally's conclusion: 'If I suddenly got a big order I don't think I would take it if the terms weren't right. I'd have to buy loads of stuff and get some additional equipment, and employ at least one person. I could do that on a temporary basis, but that's a lot of cost. I would have to negotiate very favourable payment terms – probably 40 or 50 per cent up front. I would work the numbers out in detail, and then make sure that the advance payment covered all my costs. If it did, then I would consider it, provided that it did not compromise the rarity value of my dolls. Either way, I would not be afraid to say no, which puts me in a good negotiating position.'

Cash and profit business models

Draw the business models for cash and profit for your own business in order to get the feel for them (see Figure 3 for an example). They do not have to be in fine detail; the aim is for you to see the shape of them, and know how wide or narrow the profit band is compared to the cost bands, and how big the interest and tax bands are too. You will probably have to predict tax, so consult your accountant or spend time to get the calculation right. You do not want any surprises from the Inland Revenue!

Figure 4 shows two businesses with very different shapes as far as profit goes. One is a services operation; the other is a factory. One has no borrowings; the other has an overdraft. They both show profit over a 12-month period.

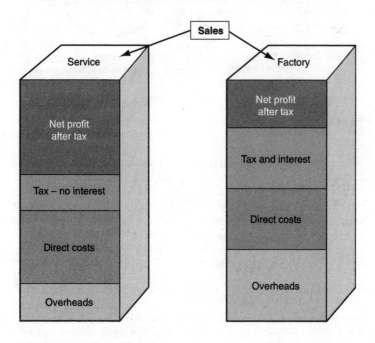

Figure 4 Profit comparison

Now consider your cash position today, and compare it with these same two organizations in Figure 5:

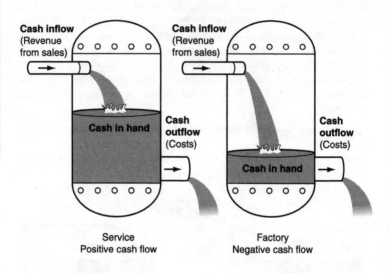

Service
Positive cash flow

Factory
Negative cash flow

Figure 5 Cash comparison

When you have your starting cash position, you can begin to project what will happen day by day. If you have a huge bill coming in at the end of the month, and your bank account is empty, how will you pay it? This is cash flow forecasting. It sounds a sophisticated process, which it can become, but we are talking here about getting the feeling for it so that you know from experience that there is a problem looming, rather than from staring at a spreadsheet.

If your business is 'lumpy', i.e. you get a small number of large orders erratically over the year, then sales forecasts are key to managing cash and to getting that feel for the business. If you can find a pattern over the years, that will help. You may think each year is different, but for most businesses you will find some kind of similarity – such as no orders in December or a busy spring.

Managing your cash flow

If you think of managing your cash flow as controlling the air supply to your business, this helps to understand how critical it is, yet it is often a neglected area of the business. There are two leverage points in managing cash – when you pay the bills, and when people pay you. Included in the bills will be VAT, the Inland Revenue and the bank. Clearly, the faster people pay you, and the longer you take to pay others, the better your cash flow will be.

Taking credit

However, it is not quite that simple because taking a long time to pay has to be balanced against your reputation, and the consequences of being labelled as a bad payer. You are less likely to get keen prices from your suppliers if they know they will have to wait a long time for their money – they may even add a bit on to the price when they deal with you. This may create ill feeling between you, and some people may even refuse to supply you, or ask for payment in advance.

Getting paid

Similarly, you can create friction by constantly asking for payment, even when it is due. Usually the problem is just the opposite, in that small businesses do not chase their money hard enough, and allow themselves to be pushed around, particularly by large companies.

It is a very good plan to build a friendly relationship with the person who actually pays your bills in the finance department. You are likely to be calling them often, so make it a pleasant interchange as far as you can. If they like you, they may well give you priority, and if they know you always ring the day before payment is due, they may learn to anticipate your call and actually pay the invoice on time. If payment is delayed beyond the norm, escalate your calls quickly because this may be a sign that your client's company has its own cash flow problems.

Be aware that your client may have little power over when you get paid if they are not at the top of the organization's tree and, even then, finance departments are notorious for being a law unto themselves. Understanding the way larger companies work does mean that you can lean hard on finance without ruining the personal relationship with your client – unless they happen to work in the finance department!

It is good business practice to analyse your debtors so that you can monitor any changes to their payment pattern or, if you do not like their payment pattern, take action to change it by asking for payment in advance, for example. If they remain bad payers, you may decide not to supply them, or at least threaten them with the prospect to see how they respond.

Payment terms

Much of this problem can be avoided if you have negotiated good payment terms. One hundred per cent up front is the best place to start which may, of course, be totally unacceptable to your client but begins a negotiation that is unlikely to end up at the standard 30 days after receipt of invoice, and any improvement is worth the effort. It is very reasonable to request stage payments if it takes more than a month to fulfil an order or if the order is very large in relation to your size.

Timing of expenditure

The other aspect of managing your cash flow is the very obvious one of monitoring the timing of your spend. Do you have to place a new order for stock just a month before your VAT payment is due? Thinking this way is basic good practice, but when you are busy and you normally order at the end of the month, you may not give the subject much thought.

Stock

Stock is dangerous because, if you allow it to sit on the shelf for any length of time, it is effectively using up your cash (air) supply. Think of it as piles of bank notes sitting there, doing nothing.

A measure of a really successful business is rapid stock turnover, which keeps the air supply flowing. The faster you move stock, the more you are selling. However, it is possible to apply this rule to a few items as well as to a warehouseful. This is why 'just in time' supply for manufacturing companies has become common practice; they do not want to tie up their cash in stock.

Cost reduction

You can improve your cash flow by reducing your costs, on anything from paper clips to salaries. Look at everything, including bank charges. If your business is always in credit and you have a proven track record of say, 18 months, try asking for reduced charges. If you are never in the red, and a good negotiator without a huge volume of transactions, you might manage to escape charges altogether – it has been done!

Always review your fixed costs and then look at the price and timing of your variable costs. Vigilance will pay off, and then you will not get into the habit of paying for things at certain times because that is what you have always done. Do they really need to be paid for now? Focusing on the air supply does bring a new sense of urgency to what may seem to be mundane considerations.

Increase in sales

The other, less direct means of improving cash flow is to sell more in volume and/or in value. Sales do not equal cash unless your clients pay on receipt, which works very well for a shop, but would not work well for a business consultant. Eventually, though, the consultant's increased turnover will become more cash in the bank, so a healthy profit margin is eventually a key contributor to a healthy cash position.

Summary

Cash is your most precious resource for business survival. Here are the steps you can take to protect and build it:

1 Get a feel for, or a picture of, how cash normally flows through your business.
2 When you have that feel, be on the alert for any deviations.
3 Monitor your costs – both fixed and variable. Challenge all expense – do we need it now – could it wait? Do we need it at all?
4 Plan spending to ensure that big bills do not coincide.
5 Review your pricing regularly – do competitive checks.
6 Take as much credit as you can – but not at the expense of your reputation. If you have agreed to pay in 30 days, do that, but do not pay in 20 – you could be using the money elsewhere.

7 Negotiate favourable payment terms, particularly at the start of a new business relationship. Ask for full payment against a proforma invoice for goods if you can. If you are selling services over a longer period, ask for stage payments.

8 Invoice promptly and accurately. Do not leave scope for query or an excuse for not paying because your invoice was late when the client operates a '30 days from receipt' policy.

9 Monitor your clients' payment patterns carefully. If they are bad payers, consider refusing to deal with them, or at least highlighting the problem, which will be taken more seriously if you can show a track record of poor performance.

Managing your profit

An unprofitable business spends more than it earns, which means that its costs are too high or its sales are too low, in volume or value, or both. Looking back at your profit model, you want to see a nice fat margin sitting between your cost base and your sales figure. If your margin is looking thin, there are three ways to go:

1 Costs down.
2 Prices up.
3 Volume up.

These are listed in order of ease of implementation: it is generally easier to reduce your costs than it is to put up your prices or to sell more, but it is as well to look at all three.

Reducing costs

Start by examining your internal costs – the office, your staff, stock and equipment. Can you compare them to a similar, non-competitive operation that you know which is very successful? This is a benchmarking exercise, and can be very instructive if you can see the detail on the basis of you show me yours and I'll show you mine.

Next look at external costs – your suppliers will represent most of these, but there are also financial costs. Loans, bank overdraft, and tax are the most common financial costs. If you are VAT registered, VAT should not be a consideration for profit, only cash. You collect it and you pay it, but it is not part of the structure of your business finances. If you are not VAT registered, this does not apply and VAT in the UK is an additional 17.5 per cent of cost on any purchase you make.

Any borrowings will be a drain on the business profits and, although this is an obvious statement, it can become a habit to rely on the overdraft. If you do not focus on paying off the business loan, it may just sit there, eating your profit. Assuming that you could assign some funds to this, do the arithmetic, or ask your accountant to do it, and work out whether paying off the loan faster will be better for the business than using the money elsewhere. Keep this under review – rates may change, business opportunities come and go – what is right for the business today may no longer be so tomorrow.

Tax will devour a chunk of your hard-earned profits, and it is here that it is worth investing in some good advice and not just a chat with your accountant, who is almost certainly not an expert. Whatever your legal status as a business, whether you are a limited company or a sole trader or partnership, there is a great deal of scope for minimizing what you pay to the Inland Revenue and maximizing the benefit to you and your business. Take advice and, after a time, if your advice becomes standardized, take some different advice.

Stock

You have ensured that your stockholding is at the optimal level, and walked the fine line between too much and too little. It is also vital to ensure that stock turns over as fast as possible to maxmize profit. The less time stock spends on the shelf, the more it will generate money to buy more stock and enable you to sell more.

Pricing

Start by checking on whether you can raise your prices. Do an informal competitive survey if you can, or ask a friend to do it for you. Just a few phone calls will be quite revealing and, of course, the Internet is also a wonderful tool for this. Do some research: 'I'm thinking of buying a CCTV system. How much would it cost?' or 'I need a new bath fitted. How long would it take, and how much do you charge by the hour?'

Small businesses are often reluctant to increase prices, thinking they will scare their clients away, but this is often not the case; many products and services have what is known as considerable price elasticity. This means that you can raise the price and still sell as many.

Volume

On the other hand, never assume that you will sell more by reducing prices. Unless you know that you are losing significant business to cheaper competitors, do not cut your prices. Instead, work on your USPs (unique selling propositions) – these are the other reasons why people will buy from you apart from price. If you have none, create some! Anything is better than cutting your price.

You may be able to sell your products in a new market with a different cost structure – via a website or mail order. This new market may enable you to charge higher prices, or to sell a higher volume at a reduced cost. All these options are explored in Chapter 17 which looks at different ways to increase your profit margin.

Summary

When you can see your margin line – thick or thin – and you know what drives it, then you can look for ways to increase it by:

1 Reducing fixed costs.
2 Reducing variable costs, including stock.
3 Reducing finance costs.
4 Raising prices.
5 Turning over stock faster.
6 Increasing sales volume.

Accountants may mystify you with fancy labels for things, but the basics of finance for a small business are very simple. If you build up your picture at this simple level, you will always be aware of how your business is running from both a cash and profit perspective.

Steps to success

Key Questions to ask:

1 Do I have a feel for, or a picture of, how cash normally flows through my business?

2 Am I comfortable that I know what to do to prevent the flow drying up?

3 How would I describe the difference between cash and profit?

4 How well do I monitor the timing of my expenditure?

5 Do I really feel the business need to negotiate good payment terms with my clients?

6 How promptly do I issue invoices?

7 How proactive is my method of collecting money owed to me?

8 How often do I review my profit margin?

9 Are there any unexplored soft spots in my cost structure?

10 What would happen if I put my prices up?

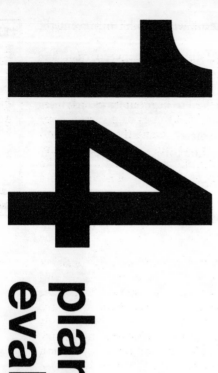

14

plan and evaluate

In this chapter you will learn:
- why you should plan
- what to evaluate
- to make planning an easy habit
- about evaluating and planning – key questions for now and the future.

'When I'm up to my neck in alligators, don't talk to me about draining the swamp!'

The above quote sums up one of the biggest problems you will ever have in running your business: you are so busy 'doing' that you have no time for thinking and planning. You have to get that order out tonight. You have to sort out that customer complaint. There are always a million things to do, and never enough time. If you are too busy just running the business and things are going well, you are certainly at risk, but if you are busy fire-fighting – dealing with problems that might look like alligators – then you are seriously at risk and you need to stand back and take stock.

Why plan?

Running out of cash is the most common cause of business failure, and it most often happens when business is good and you are so busy delivering that you have no time to chase those invoices which have not been paid yet. Never mind, you have made lots of sales and will earn lots of profit, which feels wonderfully successful. Yet when you suddenly have no money to pay staff, suppliers, rent or bank interest, you may find you have no business. In most cases this could be avoided by careful evaluation and planning, and less doing.

Running is a good word to describe what you do to a business, because often you are doing just that. Fitting in planning time may need a creative approach, and many of you will already be saying that your working day is full, although you know that planning is a big rock in your jar if you have read Chapter 11. If time is a big issue for you, be sure to read that chapter before this one.

What to evaluate

First, let us establish why you need thinking time. Below is a list of the key tasks, all of which are addressed in this book, to equip you with the elements of a business review process. Note that this list refers to running the business in its current form. There will be another list for developing or growing the business, which we will address later.

1 Get the financial feel for your business by seeing a model of profit, sales, cash and overheads. When you have that feel,

and you do not need to be an accountant to get it, it will be easy to stay in touch with it and sense any changes that might be opportunities or threats.

2 If you have any external funding for your business – from the bank, for example – review your financing and consider your relationship with them, on a personal as well as a financial basis.

3 Assess your market and how it is changing.

4 Track your competitors and what they are up to.

5 Review your clients and the business they bring you.

6 If you have staff, review their contribution, and yours to them.

7 Evaluate your suppliers and how they are performing.

8 Think about you, and how you feel about everything.

If you think this is a long list, do not worry because, if you do these things regularly, they become very manageable and, eventually, they will become second nature to you.

Making planning an easy habit

Chapter 11 will have helped you to find the time for planning. Now we want planning to become an easy habit. The key to success is to find something that feels comfortable for you, and that you can stick to. Plan to do something (but not necessarily everything), every month.

Meetings

If you think better in company rather than alone, you may want to set up a regular series of meetings with someone who will listen and may also (and this is a bonus) offer you some useful input. This could be your spouse, your business partner, your business buddy, a friend, or anyone else who fits the bill. Start off with monthly meetings and then you decrease or increase the frequency as necessary. If you can afford it, you could also pay your accountant or a business adviser to meet you, say, every quarter.

Solo time

If you think better alone, decide when you are best able to think. Before 9 a.m. or after 5.30 p.m.? At the weekend? Or can you plan to dedicate an hour at lunchtime on the last Monday of each month?

Making it a habit

Whatever you decide, find a way to ensure that you keep to it. Mark it in your diary for the year ahead, and perhaps you could plan a treat to go with it. For example, two partners of a small engineering firm go out to lunch together on the last Friday of every month, to review the business. They have nice lunches, and serious reviews. Occasionally, the date might slip, but not often, because they look forward to the lunch and find the discussions really useful.

In setting up these business review sessions, you will soon recognize how much input they require. You may meet your competitors regularly and track their progress because you consider it part of what you do. Or you may not even know who they are, in which case you will need to do some research or get someone else to do it before you hold your review.

If you are now thinking that doing the preparation for eight topics (see pages 119–20) is going to be a full-time job for you, this tells you that you are not running your business; it is running you. Lack of planning is given as the most common cause of business failure, so the old saying really does apply here: 'People don't plan to fail, they fail to plan'.

A key point about thinking and planning is that, for most people, it is hard work; much harder work than being busy delivering. This is often why we do not do it, and we have the perfect excuse – we already work far longer than we want to, simply to keep the business running. Recognize this in yourself, if it is true, because otherwise this feeling that thinking and planning is too difficult will sabotage your efforts to do it, and deprive you of the key element of your future success. Attacking the 'too-difficult' pile is covered in Chapter 11.

Evaluating and planning – key questions for now and the future

Now you have acknowledged the need for planning and found the time to do it, perhaps with some help, this section provides the questions you will be asking as you begin the process. The questions fall under the following headings:

- Financial structure
- External funding
- Market
- Competition
- Clients
- Staff
- Suppliers
- Me
- Strengths and weaknesses
- Opportunities and threats.

Financial structure

- Can I see the pictures?
- Are the pictures changing over time?
- Are the pictures going in the right direction?

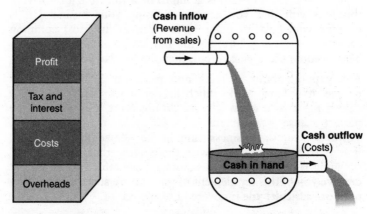

Figure 6 Financial structure

This case study illustrates the planning process. Rob has been a fencing contractor for quite some time now, and his business is chugging along. He hates paperwork and he has just found himself a business buddy who he hopes is going to make a real difference. Jane is a landscape gardener, very efficient and professional. She needs help with heavy work now and again and, in return, she has agreed to help Rob with his business planning. Rob briefed his accountant to get his figures all up to date for his meeting with Jane. This is a first for Rob, and he has in front of him data for the last two financial years (one has just ended). Jane helps him draw the diagrams, and they do not look healthy. Rob always runs what he calls 'a bit of an overdraft'. He has a pile of work for which he has not quite found the time to invoice yet, and his customers pay him in a three to six-month time frame, on average. Jane observes that this situation has become worse over the last six months. Rob's pick-up truck is almost falling apart, and he has no money to buy another. He knows that he ought to keep up to date with his paperwork, but he hates it so much.

External funding

- Am I happy with the funding arrangements that I have?
- How are they impacting on the business?
- Can I cut down my borrowings?
- Do I need to increase my funding?

Jane shows Rob that he does not need an overdraft. What he needs is prompt invoicing and swift debt collection. At the moment he is funding his customers and paying his bank for the privilege.

They discuss the pick-up truck. Rob does not intend to buy a new one, and knows where he can find a second-hand one at a good price. He decides to wait as long as possible and try to pay off his overdraft before he approaches the bank again.

Market

- What exactly is my market?
- Has it changed?
- What are the trends?
- How am I equipped to meet them?

Rob reckons he works an average of four days a week. Sometimes it is seven days, sometimes it is one. He prefers working for companies rather than for farms or private homes. Companies are easier to deal with and pay higher prices. His marketing to date has been by recommendation and by advertising in the *Yellow Pages*, the local magazine and in newsagents' windows. He has never thought of approaching companies direct. Jane sends him to look at the local industrial estates when he has some free time. He checks the fencing and, if he sees a problem, he calls in and asks to speak to the relevant person. If all looks well, he still leaves a card and gets a name to follow up later. He does the same with the bigger farms in the area, and he puts business cards through the letter boxes of houses close to home, where he can fit in small jobs most easily.

Competition

- Who are my competitors?
- How are they doing?
- What do I need to do to maintain my competitive position?
- Can I move to a non-competitive area?

Jane is surprised to find that Rob knows all the local competition – he has a drink with several of them now and again. They help each other out sometimes, pass on work that they do not want or do not have the capacity for. He knows pretty well what they charge, and how good their work is. He fits in the middle – a good workmanlike job for a fair price. The competition tends to specialize either in farm work or private housing, so his choice of company work was partly based on this knowledge.

Clients

- What is the status of my client base?
- What is their purchasing history?
- What do they think of my company/product/service?
- Do they have more or less to spend?
- Do they want anything different from me?

About a third of Rob's business is repeat, and he makes sure he has no unhappy customers, though there is rarely any issue. Clients sometimes ask him to prune back trees and shrubs 'while he is at it' and, if that is necessary for the fencing or is a very small job, then he will do it; otherwise he refers them to a specialist, which he is not, and does not wish to become.

Jane points out that repeat business invoices will be a problem, in the sense that existing clients are used to not paying him promptly. He will need to spell out new rules when he quotes any existing client.

Staff

- Am I happy with the people who work for me or work in the name of my company?

- Do staff need help, training or information to do their job better?
- What can I do to help staff become more effective and more motivated?

Rob has tried a series of bright young lads, but has not found one whose work he is happy with, so he has decided that working alone suits him best.

Suppliers

- Have I got the best suppliers?
- Is there anything I can do to make my suppliers more effective?
- Do I have back-up suppliers?
- Do I get the best terms and prices from my suppliers?

Rob has a great relationship with two suppliers of fencing materials. He knows he gets good prices, and he often checks up with his competitors. Jane points out that he could do with a better relationship with his accountant, who is simply crunching numbers on request and, in her view, should be ashamed of allowing Rob to let his cash go so far out of control with no comment. Rob tells her that his accountant has mentioned it to him, but Jane says this is not enough. Rob says he does not want to pay anyone else to do his administration, and it is clear that the business cannot afford it. Jane helps Rob work out a plan to deal with it himself, and they agree that she will ring him every week for the next six weeks to remind him and to act as his conscience. After that, he should have formed a good habit.

Me

- Am I in top form?
- Am I still passionate, focused and committed?
- Am I spending my time well – inside and outside work?
- Do I need help, support or advice?

Rob is very happy with his work, and now feels that he has the help he needs to spur him on to sorting out his administration and to growing his market to suit his preferences.

Strengths and weaknesses

- What are my business strengths?
- How can I capitalize on my strengths?

- What are my business weaknesses?
- Do I need help to address my weaknesses?
- Can I address or work round them?

Rob knows his stuff and he has a good reputation in the market, which he is now planning to build on. He buys in materials at keen prices, and his charges are carefully calculated to sit at the maximum end of his market position.

Rob is doing a good job of fencing, but he is not running a fencing business nor working on growing his current markets. He has no staffing flexibility and so there is a limit to his capacity, and a risk that his marketing efforts may produce work that he has to pass on to his competitors.

Rob has recognized that he needs help and he takes Jane's advice very seriously. He would like some help with the administration itself, but knows he cannot afford it yet.

Opportunities and threats

- Can I see new opportunities for the business?
- How can I capitalize on new opportunities?
- Do I see threats to the business?
- Can I plan to avoid threats?
- Can I plan contingencies to handle threats?

Rob has focused and capitalized on industrial site fencing, where there is least competition in his area.

Rob sees that his financial management is damaging the business and, if big expenses come in at the wrong time, he might be at serious risk. With Jane's help, he is building charts and diagrams of the key aspects of his business in order to monitor what is happening. He resolves to invoice all work within two days of completion. He will also make a list of all his clients so that he can track any repeat business and ensure that new terms are agreed. He will then monitor the timing of their payment pattern.

Rob now has a plan for getting his business back on track, and his buddy will support him. He sets himself a goal to generate enough funds to pay for a part-time administrator who, even if he can only afford half a day a week to begin with, will eventually take on all the mundane administration that he hates so much, and free Rob up to do more sales and marketing.

As Rob's example shows, these questions are all designed to help you to manage your business in its present form without thinking about taking it in a new direction. It is important not to move the goal posts when doing your evaluation. Like a house or a marriage, a business needs constant attention to keep it on top form and, if you neglect it, it will not just stand still, it will go into decline. In a business, top form does not even mean standing still, it means growing organically on its current path because if you are not growing you are almost certainly in decline, or about to head in that direction.

Planning change

When you have thoroughly reviewed the business as it currently stands, you may also decide to plan changes. This will not necessarily be because things are not going well, in fact this can often be the worst reason to change, but because you see new opportunities or you want to take the business in a new direction.

Start with an objective for change: what do you want to achieve? Change does not simply equate to a dynamic and therefore successful business. There are many ways to define success, and you are the judge, not the rest of the world. It is critical to be very clear on why you want to change before you embark on any plans.

1 Downsizing may be an option to consider. You may feel that the size of the business is no longer comfortable and you want to bring it back to a level with which you are happy so that you can take more holidays, have a better work/life balance, or just not work so hard.
2 Growth is the obvious change to make, and this can be organic – more of the same, in a new direction or by acquisition.
3 Diversification may also be a reason to change, particularly if your core market is disappearing. You cannot keep ploughing the same furrow and consequently you must rectify your course, and find different fertile soil.

The topics in the 'Evaluating and planning' section (page 121) will be a helpful basis for planning change and, indeed, they may well have sparked an idea or two already. When looking at growth, focus in particular on market, competitors, clients, strengths and opportunities, but work through each topic, because they will all drive change or be affected by it.

This chapter is an introduction to the process of planning, why you should do it, and what you can gain from it. Part 3 of this book, 'Moving on', covers how to go about developing your business: especially raising funding and preparing formal market and business plans. If you want to grow your business, you will find it helpful to read Part 3 as an extension to this chapter.

Steps to success

Key questions to ask:

1 Have you taken planning off the 'too-difficult' pile?
2 How have you structured your regular planning sessions so that they become an easy habit?
3 Are all the following under regular review?
  a Financial structure.
  b External funding.
  c Market.
  d Competition.
  e Clients.
  f Staff.
  g Suppliers.
  h Me.
  i Strengths and weaknesses.
  j Opportunities and threats.
4 Do you have recorded action plans for some or all of the areas in questions 3?

15

a passion for what you do

In this chapter you will learn:
- the passion test
- about communicating passion
- how to rekindle passion.

Most successful businesses have a driving passion behind them, and that is probably how yours began. Over time, a number of things can happen to that passion which can send your business off course, or worse. The most frequent problems associated with a faded passion for business are:

1 You find your business develops away from its origins.
2 Your role changes so that you no longer do the things that you started out doing.
3 You employ staff or use contractors who do not share your passion.

The passion test

If your passion has faded, it may well show in your business results, not to mention in you, your health or general well-being. If this has happened, it is vital to recognize it and then to understand why it has happened. It may be that things have not felt right for a while, but you cannot quite put your finger on the problem. You will not be in the habit of assessing passion levels every day, but it is worth a check now and again. Passion may not be the word you use – you may call it enthusiasm, commitment, belief, something you always wanted to do. Whatever it is, check that it is still there and, if it has diminished, or worse, disappeared, ask the following questions:

Question 1

Is the business now doing what I set it up to do, or have we taken some different direction that I do not enjoy as much?

Sarah set up as a training consultant and loved running courses, but she found that clients would ask her to do other things. Gradually she found that she spent more time at a desk and less time in the training room. Not surprisingly, her passion faded and one day she asked herself how this had happened. Through pressure from clients, was the answer, and Sarah realized that she needed to push back, to say no, or to work with a partner who would take on all the stuff she did not enjoy.

If this has happened to your business, think about how you can get back to your original operation or, like Sarah, find someone else to do the rest. If your business has changed because that is where the market is, and your original road led nowhere, then you have a far more serious problem. It is then a case of evaluating the market and your sales and marketing activities to date, and deciding if you can make it fly or whether clients are really telling you by their purchasing patterns that they no longer want what you originally offered.

Question 2

My business is still on its original track, so could it be that my role has changed and that I am now managing instead of doing?

This is a natural consequence of growth, and it may be that you talk to clients far less or are no longer involved in production. If this is the case, some careful planning is required to get you back to what you enjoy doing while at the same time, still keeping you in charge. It may sound extravagant, but perhaps you could consider employing a manager or supervisor to run the operating side of the business, while you focus on sales or production or whatever it is you enjoy. You can devise whatever structure you want, and the role of administration and co-ordination does not have to be performed by an expensive and senior person who sits at the top of the tree.

When you are doing what you do best, it will re-energize not just you but the whole operation. Someone will get equal enjoyment from their management role if you have designed it well and you have given them a balance of structure and freedom to operate in (Chapter 18 covers this in more detail).

Question 3

I still feel a passion for the business but do my staff, associates and contractors feel it like I do?

As the organization grows, it is inevitable that your passion for the business will not be shared to the same degree by all the people involved in it. The more there are, and the more remote their relationship with you, the more the passion will be diluted. Imagine the following situation:

Joanne is your new sales clerk, in a team of six, and Bill is the team supervisor. Although you have only 15 staff, you decided to give Bill the responsibility for recruiting and training Joanne. You had a quick chat with her at the interview, and she seemed fine, so you left the rest to Bill. Several weeks later, you hear Joanne on the phone to a client:

'No, I'm afraid that is not our policy. You cannot return the goods now, and we will not exchange them after 28 days. I'm sorry you feel that way, but our policy clearly states...'

It is evident that the customer has hung up on her. Bill is out at lunch, so you go over and say:

'Was there a problem there, Joanne?'

She shrugs. 'Not really. Just another customer trying it on, you get that all the time, I'm used to it from my previous job. You just have to be firm with them, that shuts them up.'

'What was your previous company's policy on complaints?'

'Well, their quality wasn't always great, so they had 14 days to return things, and if they didn't – tough luck! They always had huge campaigns running to win new customers, and if a customer started moaning, they considered them a waste of time, so we were told to get them off the phone as rapidly as possible.'

'And did Bill go through our complaints policy with you?'

'Oh yes. You allow them 30 days, which is much more generous, and he said to use my discretion and always be polite, so I'm quite happy with that.'

What do you do now, when you see that Joanne has no idea about your passion for customer care; your belief that you would rather lose money on an order than leave a customer feeling that they have been badly treated; your focus on retaining customers rather than winning new ones? As Bill is out, it is best to deal with it on the spot and say to Joanne:

'Joanne, I quite see why you dealt with the customer in that way, but it's not the way we normally treat customers. I care very deeply that every customer thinks well of us, even if that costs us money sometimes. We don't have the funds to spend on winning new customers all the time, so our aim is to keep the ones we've got. I don't think Bill explained that to you very clearly, so I'm going to talk to him this afternoon, and ask him to give you a better briefing. This is not a criticism of you. You have done all that's been asked. I just want you to know that this is absolutely critical to the way we operate, so please give it high priority – nothing matters more to me than getting our relationships with customers right, and I'm sure you'll make a good job of doing things our way, once you understand what our way is!'

After lunch, you will tell Bill what has happened, and ask him what he understands the customer policy to be, just to check that he does share your passion. If he does not, then you are seriously at fault. If he does, point out to him that he has not communicated this clearly to Joanne, and that her behaviour is his responsibility, not her error. Then he can brief Joanne and monitor her calls until he is satisfied that she shares your passion too.

To avoid this situation happening to you, the first question to ask is – do they know you have a passion at all? You might feel a little uncomfortable talking about a passion to a subcontractor, or you might never have mentioned it because it is obvious that this is what your business is about. Communicating with your people is vital; Chapter 18 covers this fully and refers specifically to the process of generating enthusiasm and commitment within your team.

Communicating passion

The foundation of enthusiasm and commitment will be when the team understands and can share in your passion. Tell them how you feel about the business, why you started it, what image you want for it and how you treat customers and suppliers. Because you are passionate about these things, they will pick up as much from the way you say them as from the words you use. Ideally, this is a conversation to be had before you hire someone, but in the real world it may come later. The important thing is that it happens, and that staff or contractors understand what standards you set and are expecting from them. If you think they will 'pick it up', then you can be fairly sure that their interpretation will not be the same as yours.

If you have done a good communication job, and there are still no positive signs, you will need to consider whether you have chosen your team well. If you face an attitude problem, the fastest way to deal with it is to part company, and find someone who shares your enthusiasm. If the person concerned is an employee, firing them can be a long road, but it much better to bite the bullet and get on with it than put up with someone who will inevitably 'infect' their colleagues with a negative approach.

Firing staff is an area where you may require professional advice – see the 'Taking it further' section for more information.

Rekindling passion

If you have considered all these options and none of them applies, something has happened to change you and cause that passion to fade. You may know this only too well. It may be that you get bored after a while and need something fresh to stimulate your enthusiasm. In this case, the answer is in your hands: how can you bring something fresh and exciting to the business? If you think you have no time for such things, consider the effect that you will have on the operation when you are feeling energized and enthusiastic – make it a priority!

It may be that you have faded in general, and are tired and worn down by overwork. Have you put too much of yourself into the business? Are you constantly worried about finances? When running your own business, it is easy to get into the overwork rut – you have to keep going, everybody depends on you, you need the money and so on. If you enjoy your work, it may not feel like work, and you can do as much of it as you like, with no ill effects.

If work has become a hard grind, it is time to take stock and think through what your priorities are. Start with these questions:

• If I died tomorrow, would I be satisfied that I have been spending my time well?

Or, to put it more positively:

• Is this what I want out of life?
• Is money more important than my health?
• Why is everything such hard work?

If you are worried about the business, be sure you are dealing with the root problem and not the symptoms. A prime example of how not to spend your time is if sales are down and, to save money, you've laid off the temp you use to send out the goods and you are doing it yourself instead. Keep the temp and focus on why sales are down and, when you know, take action to increase them. This sounds an obvious route, but burying yourself in mundane tasks can sometimes be an ostrich-type refuge, because you are too busy to deal with the real problem, which you fear you may not be able to solve. If you feel uncomfortable reading this, it is a sure sign that there is at least some sand in your eyes!

If you are worried that you cannot solve a problem, talk to your business buddy or find an expert. There is no rule that says you have to solve business problems on your own.

It may not be the business that is worrying you. It may be something in your personal life that is dragging you down. Again, it is worth asking whether you have faced the root problem and dealt with it fully. If the answer is yes, then do you need a break? 'All work and no play' is a cliché because it is true. Just staying with friends for a long weekend can be refreshing, especially if you have a long-term personal burden to carry.

If you are not worried about the business or about your personal life, there may be a physical reason why you feel so tired and lacklustre. Anaemia is an obvious cause – do a personal health check on yourself and decide if you need a second opinion from your doctor!

If you are well, with no particular worries, it may be that you are simply in the habit of overworking and feeling tired and jaded. We choose our attitude to life and work, and you may have stopped choosing. Sometimes we overwork because there is nothing to stop us. Give yourself a reason to take a night or a weekend or even a day off! Book a meal with friends, go to the cinema or to a football match. Whatever you enjoy, use it to re-kindle the passion that you had for the business, and to restore your enjoyment of what you do. If you struggle to justify time off, remember that you really will be more effective in less time if you are not permanently tired and jaded. Overworking is almost always counterproductive.

Just as you have chosen to feel tired and worn down, so you can choose to feel passionate and enthusiastic again. You can make passion a habit, and your passion will be infectious. Passion is often the thing that differentiates your business from the rest, and it is the foundation on which your success is built, which is why you should pay so much attention to retaining, disseminating and enhancing it.

Steps to success

Key questions to ask:

1 Are you doing what you love doing in the business?
2 If not, what is stopping you?
3 What if the market is driving you away from what you really want to do?
4 How do you instil your passion in your staff?
5 How do you know your staff have 'got passion'?
6 If your passion has faded, how will you get it back?

16
getting and taking advice

In this chapter you will learn:
- your views on advice
- when to get advice
- how to choose an adviser
- what to take advice on.

Your views on advice

Before going into the specifics of where to get advice on what, it is worth examining your own approach to getting and taking advice, and whether this is something you do as a matter of course or as a last resort, or not at all.

Some people feel that asking for advice is an admission of failure since you could not sort things out yourself, and weak and feeble that you are, you had to go for help. Other people would be astonished by this view, and consider getting advice to be a mark of professionalism – and therefore a strength. You would ask for advice about brain surgery or designing an airport; why not ask for advice about your own business? Just because you are a landscape designer does not make you an expert in investment funding, or taxation, so you can go ahead and ask, with no loss of face.

If you are still not convinced, you may believe that because you run your own business, you should be an expert in all aspects of it. If that is your belief, you are going to be kept very busy learning all the aspects of taxation, company and employment law, finance, marketing etc. that the experts in these fields pursue as full-time occupations – attending seminars, keeping up with current legislation and so on. Will you still be able to do justice to your core business? The likely answer is no, and you will end up with that most dangerous thing – a little knowledge.

When to get advice

It is easier to ask for advice before you take a course of action, rather than afterwards, when you discover that it did not work. Therefore, it is best to plan and this will also look far more professional.

Jack is about to set up an exclusive supply agreement with a large organization. He knows a good commercial lawyer and he arranges to see her long before he reaches contract stage so that she can advise on the negotiation and tell him what to look out for. This proves to be a much more effective and less expensive route than the one Harry took. He called in the same lawyer as Jack after he had signed a poor contract and the relationship had gone wrong.

As a general rule, if you are planning to do something new or different, getting advice beforehand means you lose nothing other than a little time and perhaps some expense, and you stand to gain a great deal. If the expense looks large to you, think of the return it will give you before you dismiss it. If it really is too much, look for alternative sources, but remember that the best consultants charge high fees because they are the best.

Choosing an adviser

There are many professionals out there, some good, some bad, all itching to offer advice and take your money. There are government sources, which may be free, and then there are friends and colleagues, one of whom may be your business buddy. The 'Taking it further' section at the end of this book is a good place to start.

Sounding boards

Sometimes it is not so much expert advice you need, as a sounding board: 'I've interviewed this girl for the telephone job, but I can't decide if taking her on is going to solve my problem because I shall still be overworked.' Someone who understands at least the outline of what you do and has a business background may be able to help you work out how to solve your problem. They will not need to do much more than ask a few questions to help you get your thinking straight: 'What problem are you trying to solve?' might be a good one to start with.

You may prefer to come up with the solution on your own, but then find that you are not comfortable with the answer. In this case, you can test it out on someone in a different way: 'There's too much work in the office, so tell me what you think of these solutions.' Your sounding board may challenge the solutions or suggest other options which you still do not like, but the chances are that they will set you off on a new track to a solution.

Business buddy

If you have chosen your business buddy well, you will have complementary skills; you can exchange your IT expertise for some financial advice, or whatever your respective strengths may be. It will be rare that you both need something from each other at the same time, but usually the relationship balances out over time and, because you are mutual advisers, it is much easier to ask what you think might be the silly questions.

'Free' advice

You may belong to organizations, such as a trade association, that offer business advice as part of the membership service. You could include banks in this category too. There is also free information courtesy of the government (such as Business Link in the UK – see 'Taking it further'). It is worth exploring what these organizations offer, and sampling them if appropriate. There is a tendency to think that if something is free it will not be very good, but that is not necessarily the case, particularly if you have paid for it through a membership fee.

Paid for advice

There are many places to go to for advice when you have money in your pocket. Start with people who are recommended by someone whose judgement you trust. Without that recommendation, it will be harder to judge the quality of what you might be getting. Naturally, professional qualifications will tell you something, but asking around is the best route. If you have a good business network around you – clients, suppliers and contacts in related fields – these are a resource you can call upon. This is vastly preferable to picking names out of the phone book.

It is also important to check on the scope of the adviser's operation. If you want tax advice, do not ask your colleague who runs the finance department of a multinational company to recommend someone. He is unlikely to have contacts with a specialist in small business taxation, and as in many areas, big business and small business can be considered separate fields of expertise.

Case study

Angela is a manicurist and she has a growing business based in the premises of her local hairdresser. She had more clients than she could cope with, even before the fashion for false nails came in, and she now employs two full-time staff. There is just room for two of them in the salon; the other employee goes to people's homes and sometimes to Angela's front room. The problem is that although demand is still growing, Angela is not really making much money. By the time she has paid salaries and rent to the salon, there is little more left than when she worked alone from home.

Angela consulted a friend who is a beautician, who told Angela that she pays too much rent and that she should put her prices up. Angela has done a little market research on pricing and she does not feel there is much scope there. She goes to see the bank manager, who also tells her that her prices are too low and her salaries too high. When she asks how to give people a pay cut, her adviser shrugs and agrees that it would be difficult.

Angela talks to her landlord about the rent, but he shows her all of his figures, and points out that they are in the very best spot on the high street. She agrees that what he is charging is fair.

At this point, Angela feels that taking advice has been a waste of time, and that she is no closer to solving her problem. Then she remembers that her accountant belongs to the local chamber of commerce. She rings her up and asks if she knows anyone who will give professional advice to small businesses: 'Why are you not asking me?' she enquires. 'Because you will tell me to put my prices up and pay less rent, like you always do!' Angela answers. The accountant gives Angela the name of a specialist small business consultant, Tom. She rings Tom and explains what her problem is. He quotes her a very reasonable fee for a half-day consultation, during which he will go through all aspects of the business, and offer some recommendations at the end of it.

They meet, and Tom systematically goes through all aspects of Angela's operation from fashion trends to inventory, and then makes several recommendations. He notes that all of Angela's team vary in the time they take to do a manicure or a pedicure. Angela is fastest, but Janine is faster than Sylvia. Angela has told both of them what their target appointments are for a day, but they are generally not achieving this target. He discusses with her the possibility of linking their pay to performance, and introducing a bonus scheme. She could even reduce their base pay, while giving them the opportunity to earn more through the bonus. This would need careful handling, both with her staff and in the calculations, but with their agreement it could be done.

He talks her through pricing, and points out that if she still has a very high demand, that would suggest that she can put her prices up. He takes this to the extent of suggesting that if she worked from home with no staff and doubled her prices, she could make more money than she does now, even assuming she only works for 70 per cent of the time. They go through how she could structure her price increase, and even offer regular customers an incentive to buy a block of appointments in advance at the old price, before the increase takes effect. Talking the pricing through in detail makes her feel confident about how she could do it and feel comfortable. Although others had given her the same advice, she needed the 'how' as much as the 'what' in order to make it happen.

Tom and Angela discuss premises and the costs of turning her living room into a salon; the effect of location; the possibility of renting less space from the hairdresser; and the cost of renting from a salon in a cheaper location.

At the end of the meeting, Angela has a good deal of research to do, and will arrange to see Tom again when she has all the information she needs to decide which way to go. She is delighted with the advice she has been given, and now feels confident about the future.

This case study illustrates the point that knowing what kind of advice you need is key to finding the right adviser. Until she sat down with Tom, Angela had not realized that it was advice on how to do things that she needed, as well as on what to do. People running small businesses can often be put off by 'fancy' language, and when an adviser makes a comment that seems basic to them, such as 'Are you planning to increase your capital expenditure?', this may alarm anyone who does not know what that means, and thinks they would look stupid if they asked.

Ideally, find an adviser who talks your language. If they do not, ask them for explanations. You can be clever if you like, and ask questions such as: 'How would you define a capital item in this context?' This question does not imply that you lack the basic understanding of a capital item, and you will still get the reply you want: 'Well, in this context I mean your car, and your office equipment.'

In reality, it is far better to risk losing face than to risk not obtaining the information you need. If you do not know what a capital item is, so what? Many experts do not realize that they are using jargon, and they will happily explain when asked.

What to take advice on

It is obvious what to take advice on if you have a specific problem, but since you are going to be proactive and not reactive about advice, you will want to make a list of potential areas and then decide if and when you need to consult.

Taxation

At some point, every business needs tax advice from a specialist, which does not normally mean your accountant. You would not go to your doctor for a spot of brain surgery, so why would you expect your accountant to be a tax expert? In both cases, the disciplines are related, but quite distinct. Your accounting firm may have a tax expert, but he or she is most unlikely to be your particular accountant.

Finance

Your accountant should be capable of advising you on the state of your business and commenting on risks and threats, such as low stock turnover or poor cash flow.

You may want to take specialist advice on debt collection and credit control techniques. Everyone assumes that they know how to get their invoices paid, but there is quite an art to dealing with difficult customers. This becomes an even more esoteric skill when you have to cope with a company going into liquidation and, as in many difficult situations in business, there is no rule that says you have to cope on your own.

Business planning

If you are going to make any major changes, and certainly if you require funding for them, you will need to prepare a business plan. If the plan is just for you, it still needs to be an accurate projection of the impact of the change on the business so that you can make the proper judgements about the decision. If the plan is for potential investors, it needs to impress them, as well as telling an honest story in an attractive way.

Funding

Advisers can help you to find business angels or major investors, bearing in mind that it can be harder to raise a small amount than a few million!

Risk management

Insurance features at the top of the risk management list, but it is worth doing a cost benefit analysis to make sure that a particular policy is worthwhile. Companies will try to sell you a policy as a 'must have', which in some cases may be the case. As a domestic parallel, you would not drive an uninsured car, but you do not necessarily need to insure your washing machine against breakdown. Talking to insurance specialists may not give you an entirely unbiased view, but your network of contacts in similar businesses to your own may tell you far more.

Another way of reducing your risk is to sell your invoices to a factoring company so that you do not have to deal with bad debt. This comes at what, for many, is too high a price, but it is worth exploring this option since the risk reduction may be worthwhile for your company.

Legal

Anything that involves employment law merits proper advice. Where sales and supply agreements are concerned, a legal expert can advise you not just on the contract itself, but also, and more usefully, on the negotiation process that leads to the contract.

Property

You may need advice on investment strategy, risk, funding and taxation as much as on the property itself, and on the relevant health and safety legislation.

Marketing

This covers many areas – advertising, public relations, research, brochures, direct mail, exhibitions and websites. There are specialists in each area, and the best adviser is one who will give you an honest opinion as to whether any of these marketing areas will work for you. It is easy to get carried away with marketing activity which feels great at the time but actually does not translate into sales.

Sales

The specialists you are most likely to find here are telesales companies (who may also call themselves telemarketing). This can be an effective route to more sales, depending on the nature of your business. You will also find small business specialists who advise on the selling process more generally, including exports, and who can advise you on the specifics of your operation.

IT

If you are not computer literate, find a friend, colleague or buddy who is before you go to the experts. Many experts will blind you with 'science', often not deliberately, but because they talk in 'techno' speak and you will need a translator.

Manufacturing

This is a huge area, and there are industry experts to call on in each field who will know about the latest process software available, for example.

Inventory control

If you have a good financial adviser, they will have told you that managing your stock well can have a dramatic effect on your business. For example, the secret of a company like Dell, the computer supplier, is that they turn over their stock in days, rather than over weeks or even months, and this makes them highly profitable.

For ease of reference, here is the list of key areas again, so that you can check off each one, to see if you could learn or improve your business by investigating the areas most relevant to your operation.

1 Taxation.
2 Finance.
   a Debt collection.
   b Credit control techniques.
3 Business planning.
4 Funding.
5 Risk management.
   a Insurance.
   b Factoring.
6 Legal.
   a Employment law.
   b Contracts.
   c Health and safety.
   d Patents/Copyright.
7 Property.
8 Marketing.
9 Sales.

a Domestic.

b Overseas.

10 IT.

11 Manufacturing.

12 Inventory control.

The true advice test is to ask yourself: 'Do I have knowledge in breadth and depth about this area?' Take funding, for example. If you have raised funding recently for three different companies using three different methods, you may not need advice in this area. If the only funding you have ever had is a bank overdraft, do not assume that you can buy a new van for a good cash price by 'just extending the overdraft'. You need a loan, not an overdraft, for a capital item but, if you were to lease the van, that would be different. This small example demonstrates that it is easy to think you know about something, when in reality you have only the narrowest experience.

It may seem expensive at the time, but buying half a day's advice from an expert may produce a serious long-term pay-off, which might mean the difference between going under and surviving.

In the 'Taking it further' section at the end of this book, you will find some specific information, together with a list of general advisers, who may be useful only as a source of where to get advice but that makes them a good place to start.

Steps to success

Key questions to ask:

1 Am I happy with the idea that asking for advice is a sign of strength, not weakness?

2 What will I have to do to ensure that I get advice before, and not after, the event?

3 Do I have a buddy, colleague or friend to talk to about whether I need advice?

4 Do I have a list of the areas for which I might need advice?

5 Do I know where to start looking for an adviser?

17 a feel for the market

In this chapter you will learn:
- how to define and analyse your market
- about expansion and diversification
- about pricing strategy
- about marketing methods

It is possible to be successful in a market without really understanding the reasons why. This is fine when sales are rising, but markets change and you may find that people are no longer buying from you. Alternatively, you may want to diversify, and it will be hard to predict success if you do not know why you were successful in the first place.

What is your market?

Some people have a natural feel for their market. They can predict general trends in ladies fashion or in management thinking. This is a real talent, to be fostered if you have it or you know someone who has it. Other people are specialists in a niche area, which may be way outside the mainstream, but they target the narrow group that occupies this niche, and form themselves a loyal customer base.

Not everyone has niche expertise or that special feel for the market but, if your business has been running successfully for a while, you are obviously addressing a market need well. The problems arise when you change or the market changes. Markets may evolve through changing taste and purchasing patterns, or the changes may be driven by your competitors. If you are not close to your market, these changes may take you off guard, and your customers may start to disappear. It is therefore vital to explore precisely what it is that your customers are buying from you – it may not be what you think you are selling. This is particularly true of services, as illustrated in the following case study.

Case study

Jane is an electrician and she always has a full diary. Finally she decides to take on some help, and Joe comes highly recommended. Jane is surprised to find that she meets some resistance to Joe from her regular clients. Eventually she discovers that, apart from a good electrical service, she has been selling the feeling of security that she gives her female clients who value having a nice friendly woman do the job, rather than a potentially threatening man. She also discovers that, as a woman, people assume she is more reliable and meticulous than a man. This comes as something of a surprise, as Jane had imagined she would have to work harder at convincing people that she could do as good a job as a man.

It did not take long for Jane to find this out by talking to her clients, but she was only provoked to do so by the change in her market offering, in the shape of Joe. Now that she understands what people are buying from her, she has the opportunity to capitalize on it, perhaps by hiring a female apprentice. If she decides to stick with Joe, she knows what she needs to address, and she can work with him to ensure that he is seen as reliable, meticulous and unthreatening too.

Defining your market position

If you ask a selection of clients what it is they like about your product or service, listen carefully to everything they say. Here is a selection of sample responses:

'Well, you always seem to have something new in the shop, I like to come in and explore. Everyone's so friendly and helpful, and nobody ever minds if you don't buy anything.'

This customer is buying from your broad range of stock, and they are also buying a friendly service, almost a community feeling, and a real pleasure in the process of shopping.

'I like your prices – cheap and cheerful. I know what I'm getting, and I know they won't last, but for what you charge I can afford to throw them away, and come back for some more.'

This customer is buying on price, and they feel that they are getting an honest deal and are not being fooled into thinking that they are getting quality on the cheap.

'Your website is really easy to use; considering you are selling complex technology, you make it simple for the amateur. Your delivery time is excellent, and you have a human being at the end of the phone for queries! I was so grateful to speak immediately to a real person! I could probably buy cheaper, but it's not worth the risk when I know you will look after me so well.'

This customer is buying excellent customer service, which is far more important to them than price. Although this is an Internet sale, they feel that someone is holding their hand all along the way.

If you asked the owners of these businesses, they might tell you that they sell crafts, kitchenware and computer peripherals, but talking to their customers reveals that they sell a great deal more than that.

When you have a definition of what you are selling, the definition will contain the following five elements. We use Ken's Kitchenware Company as an example to illustrate each element.

- **Product or service** – kitchenware
- **Price positioning** – low end
- **Market position** – honest cheapness/bright cheerful image but absolutely no frills
- **Target clients** – not just those who cannot afford anything better; includes those with an eye for a bargain, or those who will buy and throw away
- **Service** – minimal; people do not expect to pay for extras, but like good displays, clear pricing, no empty shelves and good checkout service.

The five elements will help to give you a picture of the business you are in.

Expansion and diversification

If you feel you have got the most out of your current market and you want to expand or change direction, you can go two ways:

1 Sell the same thing to a new market.
2 Sell something new to your current market.

Either way, the change needs to be consistent with everything you are selling. If Ken the kitchenware supplier decides to offer highly priced, high-quality goods, this will confuse his customers. If he decides to offer cheap and cheerful gardening products, they will be delighted.

Ken could open a different store to sell quality goods in a different location. He would probably want to use a different name, but then one would begin to ask why he was bothering to do that. To exploit his knowledge of the kitchenware market might be the answer, but he may find the buying habits of high-end consumers are not the same as their bargain hunting counterparts, and then he has lost any synergy with his current business. If his new clients find out that he also sells 'rubbish', they will not buy from him, no matter how high class his new establishment. If his old clients find out he is selling expensive stuff, they might be worried that his prices are going up, and start to look elsewhere.

Ken would do better to expand into other domestic areas, such as the office or the garden, or to expand geographically by opening more kitchenware shops. Alternatively, he could consider going into mail order, or selling through a website, though the postage costs on bulky plastic items might take the edge off his pricing advantage. All of these options build on Ken's current success. The last thing he wants to do is to start from square one in a new market, or to go into a market that jeopardizes his existing business.

When deciding on expansion or diversification, here are the key questions to ask:

1 What business am I in?
2 Can I offer my business to different clients?
3 Can I do something different for my current clients?

Market research

The answers to the last two questions above will be supplied by clients and prospects, as well as by your own views. How you get those answers needs careful planning. Clients, in particular, have the very human tendency to be nice to their suppliers. Consequently, when you ask if they would be interested in your new product, they may say yes out of politeness. The best way to avoid this problem is to get a professional to do the asking. By doing this, you will gain anonymity and, importantly, so will the respondent who is free to be really honest. The professional will ask unbiased questions, giving you accurate data, which is essential for you to be able to make good business decisions. There are many professional research organizations that will gladly come and conduct a survey for you. These organizations will offer either quantitative research, which is facts and numbers based, for example, the figures on how many people order takeaways once a week; and/or qualitative research, which is about individuals' views, motivations and opinions, for example, they might ask 'How does ordering a takeaway pizza make you feel?'

Quantitative research almost always requires a large number of people to be surveyed (minimum 100) in order to achieve reliable results, whereas qualitative research relies on spending longer talking to a smaller number of people. As a small business, particularly in the service sector, you are more likely to need qualitative research. There are many independent research consultants who will be able to offer you a more tailored and often more affordable service than most of the larger, generalist market research agencies. You may feel that you have managed so far without professional help in this area, so why use it now? The key to needing professional help is whether you know which questions to ask of which people, and how to ask. This may sound obvious, but effective market research requires specialist input to avoid the worst possible outcome – misleading research data.

If you do nothing else, seek out an appropriate professional and pay for a half day of their advice to find out what questions to ask, in what order, in what context and by whom. Even if you cannot afford to pay the professional to actually conduct the research for you and interpret the results, you will at least have some safe questions and some guidance on appropriate methods.

In some very innovative markets, particularly consumer markets, customers often do not know what they want, and will only follow a market trend when it is well established. In this case, you have to find the early adopters, the trendsetters, and ask them what they think. This is a particularly specialized research field and, if you really are about to launch something that is truly innovative, professional research advice becomes essential.

If, on the other hand, you offer a service to just a handful of clients, you may be able to glean something from them yourself by asking carefully phrased questions, such as:

- 'What are your key challenges at the moment?'
- 'How do you think your needs might change in the future?'

These questions are completely open – that is, designed to gather as much information as possible by avoiding the possibility of a yes or no reply. Only after you have asked for their ideas, without any input from you, will you then be more specific:

- 'I'm thinking of extending my service to include ... Would that be of interest to you?'

If they say yes, follow up with:

- 'To give me some idea, would you want that kind of thing very soon, or maybe in a year's time?'

This last question is designed to test the strength of the client's interest. As they know you, they will be polite and probably say yes they are interested. Asking them about timescale enables you to check on how real that interest is – the sooner they want it, the more likely they are to buy it. Yet remember that it is likely they are still being polite, and treat whatever they say with caution.

Asking clients and prospects what they want seems a straightforward business, but it is fraught with invisible problems that need professional input. Because the problems are not obvious, the need for advice is not obvious, but it will pay off. See 'Taking it further' for sources of advice and for information on market research organizations.

Expanding your current market

Case study

Sally makes pottery dolls. It is a specialist niche, and she has used her front room as a shop for a few years. She has a sign at the end of her lane to advertise her business. Sally lives in a tourist area and she has done quite well in the season. Now her children have left home, she wants to grow the business. She decides that she really likes making dolls and she does not want to go into the general pottery market, where there is a lot of competition. Her challenge is to reach a bigger piece of her existing market. Sally considers the options:

1 Open a shop in the nearby town.
2 Take a market stall.
3 Sell her dolls through other pottery shops across the county or even the country.
4 Go to craft fairs and shows with a stall.
5 Create a catalogue and sell her dolls by mail order.
6 Build a website and sell her dolls through that.
7 Sell her dolls on eBay.com or a similar shopping website.

Sally has very little money and she does not want to borrow any, and this limits her options immediately. She also wants to be based at home and she does not like the idea of too much travel – this eliminates the shop and the market, and probably craft fairs. Sally decides to do a simple trial – she puts a couple of her dolls on ebay; one for auction, and one for immediate purchase. She is surprised by the result and, after a few rapid sales and some queries from purchasers, she realizes that she has the opportunity to create a collection of dolls, rather than her current restricted line of six items. She could set up her own shop on ebay.com or build a website. She could also consider partnering with an existing mail order catalogue to minimize her outlay, but they would have to match her style, which is really rather special, and of course they would take a big cut of the profit.

We will leave Sally with this happy dilemma. Now faced with so many different routes to market, she is going to make financial decisions about investment and partnering, but also market decisions about her range and how exclusive to make it: whether to have limited editions of her dolls, which she could charge much more for; or whether to go for lower value, higher volume sales. Sally knows that unless you have a huge marketing budget to spend, it is almost always easier to sell high value than high volume.

Pricing strategy

This brings us to a key aspect of your feel for the market, which is where to pitch your price. In some markets, this is relatively easy because there is a 'going rate' for a plumber or a sandwich or an office chair. Rule 1 of pricing strategy is to find out what that going rate is. When you know it, then you can decide where you want to pitch your product or service. The Internet can be invaluable for this. If you make sumps for aquaria, for example, just pop that into your Internet search engine, and you will find your competitors and, if not their prices, an easy way to phone and get them. In Sally's case, however, there is no readily comparable product, so she will have to look at pottery vases or other similar items to see the charges for limited editions or originals.

Armed with all the information you can find, rule 2 of pricing is to never underprice. There is a widespread belief that the cheaper a product is, the more people will buy on the principle of 'pile it high, sell it cheap'. This is often true of commodities, like soap powder, where the price is well known and the bargain is well, and probably expensively, advertised. These circumstances are unlikely to apply to small businesses; if you are going to make a pricing mistake, go too high, not too low. It is much harder to increase your prices than to reduce them. If Jane the electrician (page 147) had known what her clients were really buying from her, she could have charged premium rates. As it was, she thought that as a female electrician she needed to be cheaper than the norm, and now she cannot raise her prices too much without upsetting her existing clientele. She will get there eventually, but how much better it would have been if she had researched her market in the first place.

Another reason to avoid pricing too low is that people believe that you get what you pay for. If your service or product is cheap, then it must be low quality. Availability is another factor here. If you have more interior design business than you can cope with, you might hire someone else, or put your prices up. Consultants or tradespeople have often been surprised to find that although they as much as double their daily rates, people still keep buying!

In Sally's case, there will be a limit to the number of dolls she can make because she has dismissed the idea of having someone else produce them. This therefore means that she will charge a premium for her dolls. It is possible for her to test her pricing on eBay to some extent, and she might try placing some limited edition dolls in an expensive gift shop in her local town on a sale or return basis at the highest price they will agree to. This should give her some idea of where to pitch her prices. Having a limited edition range and a 'regular' range enables her to occupy two price points, which gives her more flexibility.

Rule 3 of pricing is to never assume that it is your price that is preventing the sale. When sales do not happen, it is easy to blame price, but that is rarely the real problem. Try everything else first, before you touch the price!

Review of marketing methods

If you have a very small number of clients, you only need to add one or two more for significant market expansion. If your mail order catalogue already reaches 1500 people, you obviously need to reach many more for serious expansion. There are many different marketing ways to achieve this goal of expansion, depending on the type of business and your route to market.

Selling

The first marketing method is to sell directly. This may seem so obvious that it is hardly worth mentioning, yet it has, for many, a bad reputation either as a 'foot in the door' activity or as too difficult. There is a tendency to do other things, like build a website or send out direct mail, which are probably less effective because there is no substitute for direct selling unless you are dealing with such large numbers of clients that it becomes uneconomical.

It helps, when selling, to ask the question, 'How am I solving my client's problem?' This works particularly well for services, as illustrated by James, a strategic planning consultant. He can ring a corporate finance director and say: 'I'm a specialist in strategic planning, and I know that the new laws on corporate governance are creating headaches in the boardroom – I wonder if you are facing similar problems?' If the answer is in any way positive, he can suggest that he may be able to help, and suggest a preliminary discussion. This technique works less well for Sally and her pottery dolls, unless she is solving a gift problem for someone: 'What shall I buy my sister for her birthday?' or even 'What should I put on my mantelpiece?' Alternatively, she could be solving a problem for the shopkeeper: 'Are you looking for new gift ranges?'

Where it does work, direct selling casts the seller in the role of helper, and that is a much easier conversation to have than pushing your offering at someone who you fear does not want it.

Networking

In Chapter 20 on business relationships, there is a list of all the different people and organizations you might get leads from for your business. If you are always alert to the potential of any business relationship, you can find leads anywhere. The most obvious places are your current clients, your colleagues, advisers, suppliers, investors and surprisingly, in some areas, your competitors.

Recommendations and referrals

If your business expanded purely through the recommendations of your clients, what a lovely business it would be. Sometimes this happens naturally: 'I came for a pedicure because my friend said you were really good.' Sometimes you need to help things along a bit. 'Do you know anyone else who would be interested in my services?' Either way, recommendations are precious, and the very best way of growing your business. It is definitely worth offering an incentive to anyone who could be a source of leads for you. For example, James the strategic planning consultant knows various HR consultants, and they have a mutual agreement that they will give 10 per cent of their initial fee for any successful introduction.

PR

Sally gets lucky with her production of pottery dolls. A holidaying journalist drops in, and loves the dolls. She asks Sally if she can feature her in a piece she is doing on regional pottery. And would she be interested in doing a special offer for the national woman's magazine she writes for? This is worth far more than advertising and, needless to say, the offer is way oversubscribed. Sally is glad she insisted that it was a limited edition of 200 only, and that she did not compromise too much on price.

If you can get any kind of press coverage, and if it is linked to sales as in Sally's case, it is well worth the effort. It costs you nothing except time. It is unusual to have a newsworthy product, as Sally does, but it can be worth approaching the sorts of magazines that your target prospects would read, if you can think of an interesting angle on your product or service. Jane the electrician might find some interest in the challenges she faces as a female electrician, for example. She would want this coverage in her local paper, or in whatever area is her target market. If she is lucky enough to get national coverage, she may get local coverage too.

The alternative way of getting coverage is to write an article yourself. Think of an angle – for example, a new idea for conservatory decor – then talk to the relevant newspapers or magazines to see if they are interested. If you get a nibble, it is worth writing the article to meet their specification and, while you will not be able to advertise too overtly, you will write something designed to attract new clients, with your contact details given at the end.

The list of expansion marketing methods so far has incurred no cost, apart from your time. Now we come to the many methods which require you to reach into your pocket!

Telesales

You could do this yourself as the first part of direct selling; the name 'telesales' usually applies to using an agency to make the calls for you, either to set up appointments or to make a sale. Everyone is familiar with the calls about double glazing or new kitchens that we all get at home; this is teleselling at its most soulless. However, companies keep calling, which must mean that it works.

You can consider using telesales regularly, or have a blitz – say after mailing a group of prospects. It is possible to negotiate some form of payment by results with telesales agencies to ensure that you get something tangible for your fee.

Direct mail

You do not have to produce glossy brochures or catalogues to send out as direct mail. For instance, if you run a carpet cleaning business, you could pick a slack period and send out a simple printed postcard to a local area, offering a discount for a set period. You could buy a list of names from the many organizations that trade in them, or you could set up a deal with the post office to deliver to a number of postcodes. There are many ways of handling direct mail, but bear in mind that response rates are very low – often under 1 per cent – so your coverage needs to be high and your list needs to be good. Be very clear about what group the list claims to target – they vary enormously in quality of entries. The lists also vary in how up to date they are – always ask when the list was last 'cleaned'.

It also helps to imagine receiving a bundle of post in the morning, with your mailing in it. Does it stand out from the others? Does it look boring? Will it go straight in the bin, unopened? Sometimes the glossiest things are not what people notice – so a simple card might work better than a colour brochure. The key questions to ask about direct mail are:

1 Do I need to generate prospects in quantity?
2 Are my target prospects easily accessible by mail? (That is, 'Do I have, or can I buy a good target list of names?')
3 Is my product or service easy to understand?

If the answer to any of these is no, try another sales method.

Exhibitions

Finding the money for a nice exhibition stand, and then staffing it for 12 hours daily over several days takes up a great deal of resources. It is therefore vital to ensure that you will get a good return from this investment. Some exhibitions allow selling to take place. If you are a specialist in potholing equipment, and you can go to the annual Potholersfest in Munich every year where all the world's potholers go, and sell your stuff at the same time, it is almost certainly worth it. Even without the sales opportunity, it might be worth it if this really is the big exhibition for your niche and everybody goes there. If exhibitions in your specialist area happen four times a year, in all the countries of Europe, you will probably not be rushing to Munich, and maybe not to any of them.

If you are a management consultant specializing in strategic planning for multinational companies, you are unlikely to consider an exhibition as a useful marketing tool. To start with, it can be quite difficult to demonstrate a service but, more importantly, it is unlikely that someone from the board of a multinational is going to pop into an exhibition to look for a strategic planner.

Beware of going to exhibitions because your competitors go. If it is the only exhibition for your niche, this may be a valid concern, but otherwise think hard about how much business you might generate for a significant outlay. Many exhibitions produce a pile of business cards and a large number of time wasters. Most of the business cards will not make it past lukewarm leads, so keep checking 'Is it worth it?' The key questions to ask about exhibitions are:

1 Is this the only exhibition relevant to my business?
2 Can I sell there?
3 How much would I need to sell to offset the full costs of attending?
4 If I used the exhibition money in some other way, could I sell more?

Advertising

If you have a niche, find the specialist publications and advertise in them. Nigel puts his handmade hives into *Beekeepers' Health and Fitness* magazine in the appropriate season, and he gets a regular flow of orders for a very reasonable cost.

James, our strategic planning consultant, does not advertise. He only works with a maximum of three clients at any one time and they would not look in a professional journal to find his services, and he certainly would not consider the cost of something like the *Financial Times* to advertise, even if he thought it was appropriate.

Henry, however, provides a local car valeting service, which he advertises regularly in the community newsletter, and with cards in all the local newsagents. Sometimes he puts a little ad in the local paper, but only for a special offer.

If the advertising is tightly targeted, it will almost certainly be relatively cheap and, therefore, cost-effective. If the cost of advertising is high, it is almost certainly not worth it for a small business, unless you are planning to launch a product in a big way.

Website

Websites fall into two types:

1 Those that trade.
2 Those that offer information.

Whichever you choose, a website is becoming a staple business requirement, like a business card. You can manage without one, but if you want to appear as a convincing presence in your market, you need one. If you have made that decision, it is important to decide how much to invest. Unless you are a computer genius in your spare time, do not be tempted to build the site yourself, just as you would not build your own desk or design your own logo. You may be able to do these things but, if they are not your core business, it is better to get an expert to do a professional job while you are earning your money doing what you are good at.

A website involves two sets of people: those who design it; and those who build it. Some do both, but do be aware that these are quite diverse skills, which do not often reside in one person. Similarly, you need to find someone with a track record in building trading sites if you are going to be dealing in shopping baskets and online credit card payments. The good news is that there are a great many trading sites that operate extremely well, and the expertise is not difficult to find. As with all other markets, there is a range of fee levels, and it is quite possible to get a good site built cheaply by a very small company with low overheads.

Do not delegate to anyone the decisions about the key messages that you want the site to convey and which key words to register with the search engines. As with all other marketing tools, websites work better for some types of business than others. 'Potholing equipment' is a nice, specific set of keywords which a search engine like Google will love, and a good website is a must – probably a trading website would work best. 'Strategic planning', on the other hand, will not deliver good results for James – it is much too general. His decision to have a website was more strategic – to establish his market presence, and describe some of his successes. It is a PR tool, not a sales tool for him, and it projects his image of great professionalism.

'Car valet' will be much too general for the search engines too but, if someone puts a postcode next to it, then Henry's business will show up. For him, a website was a marginal decision – having the potential to generate some sales, but not worthy of much investment. He therefore has the simplest single page site, for a very low outlay. He also registered with Yell.com – the online *Yellow Pages*.

It is helpful to think about the key words that apply to your business in order to register them with the search engines. The more specific they are, and preferably concrete too, the more likely people are to find your site and to turn into a sales lead. If your key words are very general, like hardware, or abstract, like management consulting, do not expect half the Internet to beat a path to your site. In this case, you need to decide what function the site will serve, and how much to invest.

Sales agents and distributors

Sales agents and distributors can range from Sally's pottery dolls example, where she asks a shop to sell her goods on sale or return, to a complete distribution service. If you are planning to supply goods in large quantities, this may be the only way to go. Be aware that distribution does not mean selling, yet it does mean taking quite a big slice of your margin. Generally a distributor simply distributes, and if the goods do not sell, they will tell you that it is your problem because your product is too expensive or not attractive enough, or whatever other problem they can lay at your feet. As long as you understand that, and the fact that this may not be made clear at the start of your relationship, this arrangement can work well.

Staff agencies

If you are selling a service, you may consider using agencies of various kinds to find you work. The most well known are the IT agencies that supply the contract market, but there are many others specializing in such things as interim management, coaches and trainers. Staff agencies take a significant chunk of your fees, to take away the hassle of finding business, but you will need to manage the agency in order to keep your profile high enough to obtain work.

Seminars

This is primarily a tool for the business market, where you have a product or service around which you offer some educational content. The seminar can be free, or at a token very low price. The deal for the prospect is that they learn something useful at little or no cost. In exchange for that, they recognize that you will be treating everything that surrounds the input as a sales opportunity. If you put too much sales into the content, they will get very upset because you are not offering truly useful information, just a sales pitch. However, if you sell to them at coffee breaks or over lunch, that is part of the deal.

This is an effective sales tool when you have something very new or different to say – as judged by your prospects, not by you! If this is not the case, you can spend more time setting up a seminar and trying to pin down attendees, than you would have done by simply cold calling each one.

Whatever method you choose for your expansion programme, be sure that it will deliver a return on your investment. It is so easy to get carried away in producing beautiful marketing material, of whatever kind, only to find that your prospects do not share your enthusiasm, and a great deal of money has been wasted. As a general rule, when in doubt, sell directly or only do things that guarantee a return.

Steps to success

Key questions to ask:

1 Do I know what my customers are buying from me?
2 How is my market changing?
3 What moves are my competitors making?
4 How do I obtain the market research information I need?
5 How often do I review my pricing strategy?
6 What are my market goals?
7 What marketing methods will best enable me to meet my goals?
8 How would I test each method?

18

getting the best from your people

In this chapter you will learn:
- about culture and values
- about recruitment and selection
- how to train and develop staff
- how to set goals and standards
- about motivation and assessment.

This chapter tells you how to get the best from your people, whether or not they are directly employed by you. If contractors play a part in delivering your product or service to your clients, then they qualify as 'your people', and it is vital to recognize this point when staff are not your employees. Remember that they are just as much representatives of your company, whether you subcontract them for a regular service or pay them for occasional temporary work. Everything in this chapter will apply in some degree to all your people, not just to those on your payroll.

Culture and values

You may not have given culture and values much conscious thought, but your company has both, and staff will learn what they are either because you tell them or by experience. Sometimes staff will work things out correctly; sometimes they will get the wrong message and they may pass this on to your clients, as we saw in the company profile in Chapter 7. Here, Jeff and Barry recruited two people, Amy and Garth, who they believed shared their passion for training. However, the owners' passion was delivering customer service through training, whereas Amy's and Garth's passion was performing well in front of their trainees. This failure to detect the difference in values had almost disastrous consequences for the company.

Case study

Contrast the small modern manufacturing unit (MMU), clean, tidy and efficient, with the same operation in a lean-to shed (LTS), in permanent chaos, but apparently producing the same result. In fact, MMU produces goods promptly and cheaply, but using inferior quality materials. LTS, on the other hand, produces goods at a fair price, of the highest quality, but not always on time.

The values of MMU are efficiency, punctuality and cheapness. This is reflected in the culture. The company wants staff who are efficient and punctual, and although it does not pay them badly, it is a quite a hard taskmaster – staff are expected to keep their noses glued to the grindstone during the working day, and working there is not much fun.

The values of LTS are quality and value for money. This shows in the company culture, where staff are given a great deal of freedom and have a lot of laughs, but they know that ultimately they have to do a high-quality job in a reasonable time in order to produce a value for money result. An employee transferring from one company to the other would have quite a few adjustments to make to meet the values and culture of their new employer, and might easily mistake the chaos of LMS for permission to produce shoddy workmanship – the very opposite of what the company stands for.

If you are not clear what your culture and values are, now is a good time to identify them, and do be honest with yourself, because you will not fool anyone, least of all your staff, by coming up with what sounds good. Many large corporations state glibly that 'People are our greatest asset'. Their staff will often tell you that this is not true at all, and that 'Profit is all that matters,' would be a more honest statement.

Common values

Here are some of the most frequently occurring headings under which values are defined:

- Customer satisfaction
- Ethics/integrity
- Respect for others
- Open communication
- Profitability
- Teamwork
- Innovation/change
- Community service
- Social responsibility
- Security/safety
- Employee job satisfaction
- Having fun!

When you have identified your six top values, put them in order and really test them by asking yourself questions such as: If you were forced to choose, would you rather have an unprofitable sale or an unhappy customer?

Communicating values

When you are clear, think about how you will communicate your values to someone new to your organization. Perhaps a self-employed person who will be doing occasional work for you – we'll call her Leanne, for convenience. Let's assume your key value is that outstanding customer service results in a profitable business. This also means that efficiency and attention to detail are vital, as are a friendly manner and a willingness to go the extra mile for the client.

Leanne needs to understand all this before she lifts a finger for you. If you wait until she has been off-hand with a client or made a sloppy mistake because detail does not matter to her, then you are both off on the wrong foot, and it is not her fault, it is yours! It is easy to explain to someone that 'this is the way we do things here' before they start, but much harder to do it later. Do be sure that you cover the how, as well as the what. Telling someone to answer the phone promptly and be courteous to customers does not do justice to your values. Show Leanne your passion for outstanding service so that she can share it. If she does not know about it, she will not stand much of a chance of living up to your values, and your clients will notice.

By now you will have realized that this discussion about values should happen at the recruitment stage, not after Leanne's arrival. However, let's assume that Leanne is the woman next door, who you've known for years, and only wants to do the occasional part-time packing for you. She still needs to know your values, which you may never have discussed with her before – it's so easy to think that they are obvious or that everybody sees things the way you do. You are safe in assuming that they do not. It is also important to recognize that Leanne needs this information even though she is only an occasional packer. She is still a part of your team, and although she may speak to a customer rarely, when she does, you want to be sure that the message is right.

Recruitment and selection

Now you are going to do things in the right order, and plan the recruitment process. You need to hire someone, so ask yourself the following questions:

1 Why do I need to hire?
2 Do I want to expand?
3 How else could the work be done?

4 Is the work temporary or permanent?
5 Is the work part-time or full-time?
6 If I reorganize, can I structure the job differently?
7 What exactly will the job consist of?
8 What is the market rate for this role?

You will have thought hard about what the job involves, what skills and experience you need, what the market rate for the job is, and what you can afford. If you need someone badly, but cannot afford to pay the market rate, you may consider looking for someone young and inexperienced to train them up, which is what Ronaldson Rey tried to do in Chapter 7. This might be a good solution, or it might be false economy. Do not underestimate the amount of time that training will take up, and the revenue that might be lost when training rather than earning. There is also the risk that the bright, young thing might not become the silk purse you had in mind. You will then have invested a lot of time in a sow's ear that you will have to get rid of, as we saw in Chapter 7.

Only when you are really clear about the job, can you identify the right person to fill it:

1 Do they have to be on the payroll?
2 What skills do they need? Are these essential or simply desirable?
3 What experience must they have? Suppose they have none, will it matter?
4 How much training will they need?
5 What personal qualities will they have, to match your values and fit your culture?

Think creatively about your specification. Could you settle for less in the way of experience and qualifications? Could you consider part-time rather than full-time? Could you structure the work in a different way – dividing up the skills? Or should you just bite the bullet and pay up, which could be more cost-effective in the long run if you choose the right person.

Now decide if you need any help with the recruitment process:

• A friend, colleague or business buddy to discuss the specifications and hiring process. It is essential to have someone to challenge your thinking on such an important decision.

- A paid professional to do the hiring – you may feel that this is an expensive route, but it could save you money in the long run, as illustrated in Chapter 7.

Whatever route you have chosen, there will eventually come a point when you interview candidates. Prepare for this by listing all the information you are looking for, and devising questions to get it. Do not worry about referring to your notes during the interview. There is no rule that says interviews have to flow fluently like informal chats; even though a chat may feel more comfortable, it will probably not tell you all you need to know. You may find the following checklist helpful:

- **Skills** – work out how to test these, either in practice – ask the candidate to demonstrate their packing skills, for example – or by questions like: 'If a client reports software problem X, with these characteristics, what would you do?'
- **Circumstances** – check out the practicalities carefully, such as how far away the candidate lives, and how difficult the journey will be. Take care here not to discriminate, for example, against a single mother who needs to catch two buses to get to you, but it is important to know as much as possible about each candidate before making a decision, and also to make sure that they are aware of what they are taking on.
- **Qualities** – here your list of values will be invaluable! Work out test scenarios for each one, and don't make them too obvious. Here is a sample question for outstanding customer service:

  'A regular client calls you for the third time about a product she is not entirely happy with. She has a reputation for moaning, and is generally understood to be a nuisance by the telephone team. It is policy to give refunds up to 28 days after purchase. She has had this product for almost two months, and now decides she wants a refund. You are alone in the office today, what do you say?'

A good check for culture fit is to have short-listed candidates visit the office and have lunch or coffee with the team, but you must be prepared to accept the team's veto! It is always helpful to have a second opinion on a candidate – involve someone else in the process if you can.

The law

If you do everything described in this chapter, the law will not be an issue for you. However, it is important to be aware of the kind of legislation that applies to the people in your business, particularly in the area of discrimination. In the 'Taking it further' section at the end of the book there are some useful reference sites which cover the basics. You do not need anything more than a broad appreciation – if detail becomes necessary, you will almost certainly need expert help.

Induction

Vision and values

You have made the decision, and your new employee or associate or subcontractor starts next week. Plan your time with them – at least an hour when they arrive – to tell them about your vision, your values and the company culture. They will already have heard this at interview, but say it again now, with passion! When you've said it, translate it for them into their own role: 'So when you speak to customers about packing charges, it means that...'

Standards

After values come standards – what you expect of your people, and how you expect them to interact with each other, as well as with clients and suppliers. A standard can be anything from 'We always use two layers of bubble wrap', through to 'We always stay on site until we've fixed the software.' Your standards may be very different from 'normal', which is all the more reason to explain them right at the beginning, before your new hire does what is normal, and not what you expect.

Your aim is to enable the new recruit to see where the company is going, how it behaves, how they fit in, and exactly what they have to do and how you expect them to do it in order to make the contribution you are paying them for. Do not make the mistake of showing them the coffee machine, the basics of the job, and leaving them to get on with it with the words 'Any questions, just ask!' A few people will ask, but most will think they are free to use their judgement, which may not coincide with yours.

Training and development

Depending on the type and complexity of the role, some jobs require a day's training and some will need months. The longer the training period, the more a plan is needed. Make bullet point notes on the key areas of the training then, if the programme is anything over a couple of days, ask the trainee themselves to produce the detailed plan. If your organization is big enough, you might assign a mentor to them to help them with their training and to provide information and guidance. If your organization is small, cast yourself in the role, and make sure that you are able to offer patience, time and enthusiasm.

Setting goals and standards

Whenever possible, when the main training period is over, ask the individual to draft their own goals for the job, in the context you have given them, and to bring their proposals to you for discussion. You may be surprised to find that they set themselves higher standards than you would expect, and if they do the opposite, you have the basis for a useful discussion. Be assured that they are much more likely to do the former than the latter.

Encouraging staff to set their own goals for, say, customer service, in the context of the values that you have already made clear to them, is an excellent way of winning their commitment to performance standards. This is far more effective than 'imposing' the goal on them or, worse, saying nothing until they do something wrong, and then correcting them. This last aproach can have a very demotivating effect, particularly if the recruit feels that they were not clear about what you expected. Here are two examples:

Mary is your new order administration manager. She deals with all aspects of orders, from taking client orders over the phone to handling complaints and returns. Her predecessor was pretty good and kept records of the number of complaints and details of returns, which have been pretty stable for a while.

First, you could tell Mary that her targets are that she must not exceed the average number of returns of the last six months, and that she must try to improve on that. Or, second, you could suggest to Mary that, after looking at these figures, she proposes a target for the coming year.

If you do the latter, she will not come back with 'I'll match the existing figures, and try to do a bit better if I can', because you will have recruited someone who shares your passion for outstanding customer service. She will say something like: 'I've studied the figures and in particular the reasons for returns and complaints. There seem to be a lot of problems with colour matching – if there's a way to improve on that, I think we could reduce the figures by at least 10 per cent in the next six months.'

If you think this is wishful thinking, rest assured that this is one of many real-life examples of a formula that works, over and over again. The formula reads: take one person with the right attitude; give them a clear framework within which to operate so that they know what they are doing and why; and then give them the freedom to recommend the goals for their job. You will be pleased, if not delighted, with the result.

Motivation and assessment

Following the formula for setting goals in the last section puts you a long way down the road to staff motivation. If you are wondering why you need to bother with all this management stuff, the answer is simple – motivated staff deliver more, faster and better than non-motivated staff. This is not an exercise in being nice to people for the sake of it. For once, there is a win win for all – motivated staff enjoy their work much more, and you get much more out of them at the same time.

Motivation means enthusiasm and commitment to the job and the company. It is not achieved, fortunately for most small businesses, by high pay and luxurious working conditions. It is possible to be motivated and poorly paid, working in a dungeon. It is just as possible to be demotivated in a highly paid role in a prestigious office. It helps if pay is at least fair and conditions acceptable. There is no need for lots of lavish fringe benefits, so do not waste your money on them, especially if they are a substitute for the things that really matter, which are:

- **Trust** – you talk to your staff and share with them appropriate information about the business so that they always understand what part they are playing, where you are all heading, and how the journey is going.
- **Respect** – this is best shown by asking for and then listening to the views of your staff – taking what they say seriously. You will get better quality input if your team are well

informed and if you make it clear that you expect them to think about the business and offer their ideas.

Goals

Imagine running a race without knowing where the finishing line is. Staff gain great satisfaction from seeing clearly what they have to aim for, and then by getting there.

Recognition

When your staff reach the finishing line, or have just overcome a huge obstacle, be sure to tell them how pleased you are. People vary enormously in how much feedback they need from others. If you have set up your own business, the chances are that you can survive on very little feedback. However, be aware that most people are not like you, and some need praise and encouragement like they need air to breathe. You can transform someone's day by saying something very simple like 'That went really well, Lisa.' If this does not come naturally to you, make a resolution to say something nice to someone every day – but only if you really mean it. If you say things simply for the sake of it, staff soon realize that these are empty words and ignore them.

Celebration

If something major has been achieved, particularly if it has been a team effort, celebration is another form of recognition. This does not mean lavish spending – it could be a drink in the pub, or a round of cream cakes with afternoon tea. What you spend is irrelevant, it is marking the occasion that matters, and your words of thanks and praise are the key.

Negative feedback

Just as staff want the good news, they also want the bad news. If someone has made a mess of something, they need your feedback; they need to know if you think it is as bad as they do – and you may not. They need the air to be cleared and they may need help in learning from the mistake. So deal with it at once, and in private.

Talk about specific behaviours, not personality traits: 'This report did not address the core problem' is easier to accept and more likely to be true than 'You are a lousy report writer'. Treat the discussion positively as a learning experience and ask what the employee will do next time to prevent it happening. Never leave it to fester, or sweep it under the carpet. If you do the latter, you will know it is there, but your staff may think it was not a problem at all.

It is also motivating for staff to know that mistakes are dealt with positively and, from a fairness point of view, that some staff are not allowed to 'get away with things'. Fairness is vital if you have a team of people working closely together who will always compare the way you treat them with the way you treat the others. A culture of respect is vital here too so that staff all respect each other, just as you respect each of them.

Staff development

After staff have become fully trained and proficient in their roles, it is highly motivating for them to know that you care about their personal career aims and interests. In this way, whenever possible, you can match their needs with the company needs. Sometimes these needs will not match – that is reality; if you are running a tyre fitting company and your receptionist wants to try hairdressing, you are going to part company. However, if she showed an interest in learning about book-keeping, that might be different and, even if you do not have an immediate need, it might be a worthwhile investment to help her with evening classes or to give her a little experience to see how she gets on.

You are achieving a number of things here – quite apart from being nice to your receptionist. By committing even a small amount of time and money, you are demonstrating that you care about her, and this buys loyalty, motivation and commitment. You are likely to get a more productive employee who is more interested in her work and who stays with you for longer. Eventually, you may get a new book-keeper, which would be an added bonus; you will certainly get some holiday and sickness cover. This makes sharing the cost of evening classes and a few hours' training time look like a very good deal.

Communication

Nothing is easier, in a small organization, than to assume that everyone knows what you know or, worse, that everyone knows all you think they need to know. In the first case, you commit the sin of omission; in the second case, you are not treating your staff with the respect they deserve.

If omission is your problem and you do not think to tell people things or you assume you've told them all when you only mentioned it to your co-director, the solution is to do a deal with your team. Tell them that you want to keep them in touch, but that you are not very good at it, and ask for their help. Someone could take responsibility for checking with you regularly, and then telling the team on your behalf if the information is minor. If the information is more significant, they could set up a quick meeting for you to tell the important things directly to the team, which is far preferable to second-hand information. You may not like being 'chased', but it means you have one less thing to think about, and ensures that you are doing something vital, which is keeping your staff in the picture. Again, you are not doing this to be nice to staff. Good communication generally means a more efficient operation, and makes staff feel important and involved. They also have the opportunity to comment on what they hear, which can prove invaluable feedback, provided that you give them the opportunity to do so.

Staff treated in this way are more motivated, more productive, more committed and more loyal – not a bad pay-off for a small investment of your time.

If you believe that you tell your staff all they need to know, this needs careful examination. If it means you tell them everything that is going on except your personal financial details, that is fine. If it means you tell them just enough to do their job, you are insulting them and missing opportunities, as well as creating a negative impact. The message received is that these people can only contribute in the precise role you employ them for, and no more. This means that you think they must be incapable of going further. The staff will also assume that you think that they are not to be trusted with more information, so they believe that you see them as untrustworthy, probably unintelligent, and certainly incapable of growing and contributing to the business beyond their current role.

These feelings are likely to translate into lower productivity, shorter length of service, and no attempt to go the extra mile – why should they? – you do not believe they are capable of it.

Tell staff as much as you can – you will find it is an investment of your time that will deliver a more effective, motivated and focused group of people who, because they know where the company is going, can give of their best and help everyone else to do so too. One business owner, describing how his business had almost gone under, said that it was his love for his staff and their support for him at every stage that had brought the business through the crisis.

Rewards

As we have already mentioned in this chapter, there are many things which are far more important than the amount that you pay your people. However, there are some basic rules which must be followed to ensure that pay does not work to demotivate staff.

First, pay must be fair internally. If Sheila in packing earns more than Peter, who thinks he does the same job, you need to explain this to Peter before he finds out – because he surely will. You may have good reasons – Sheila has other responsibilities would be the best one. If she genuinely does a better or faster job than Peter, he needs to know that – not just to explain his salary, but also because he needs to understand that his performance has some way to go. If he thinks he does the same job, he has a poor understanding of the standards you expect.

Second, the pay must be fair externally. This does not mean that you have to match the market rate, but you need to be somewhere near it. If you took on a junior to make the tea, and they are now doing a skilled job well, you should be paying them the rate for that job, and not a junior rate plus a little bit. They will almost certainly leave if their pay is grossly out of line with the market. As long as you are in range, they will accept pay at the low end of it, especially if they are motivated in other ways.

Third, pay is at its most motivating when it is related to performance: to individual, department or company performance. These last two might take the form of bonuses, but individual performance should be reflected in salary. This becomes quite easy to do when you have clear standards for the job, and give good feedback to your staff. They know what is expected, and they know that they will be rewarded for doing that extra mile. What is also important to them is to know that someone who only puts in 80 per cent will receive less – fairness is a key factor in any aspect of pay.

Bonus schemes

Bonus schemes can be very effective in a small business, but they must be carefully thought through. Designed badly, they can undermine team working, reward the undeserving or turn into pure cost with no real return.

An obvious scheme is to give everyone a flat amount, based on hitting a sales or profit figure for the year. If everyone who gets the bonus can really make a direct difference to that year end number, this can be a good scheme. If you have a receptionist, what can she do? If you have too many people in this type of bonus-related job, the bonus may degenerate into an annual expected payout just for being there. This is not to say that you want to exclude the receptionist – she may work doubly hard to be charming to clients and prospects and create a most favourable impression of your company – but do recognize who can contribute directly, and who indirectly, and tailor the scheme accordingly.

The scheme should not reward passengers. A brave way to deal with this is to issue a team bonus as a total, and then ask them to vote on who gets what. A good team will all vote for everyone to get the same. They will not do so if there is someone who has not pulled their weight, but in most cases the team will have addressed this issue before they get to the bonus pay out.

Review the bonus scheme often, do not let it become a habit otherwise it will lose its impact on results and its motivational effect. Once established, it can be very demotivating to staff to take a bonus scheme away, which is why every bonus scheme should be a one-off special, which you may decide to repeat, at your discretion!

In conclusion, the importance of the people who work for you cannot be underestimated. Think of them as clones of you – impossible of course, but you do want them to represent you, whether directly to clients or just in the way they pack a parcel. Everything matters to deliver the image you have created. If you have this perspective, you will take the whole process of recruitment, training and management of people very seriously. You will not be rushed into taking on the first warm body that comes through the door, or into thinking that you do not have time to spend with the office junior. Your people are so critical

to your business that you know the investment you make in
them will pay huge dividends.

Steps to success

Key questions to ask:

1 Who are 'my people'?
2 How well do they reflect my values?
3 If I need to recruit, how will I go about it?
4 How clear are my staff about their goals and standards?
5 How often do I offer praise?
6 When and how do I give negative feedback?
7 Do I tell my staff all I can, or all I think they need to know?
8 What impact does my reward scheme have on staff
performance?
9 Do I believe in my staff and their ability to contribute beyond
what I pay them to do?

19

flexibility in business structure

In this chapter you will learn:
- about your attitude to risk and security
- about contingency planning
- about financial flexibility
- about market flexibility.

Much of this book and this chapter is about security – making your business safe from financial disasters or market downturns – because this is the reason why businesses often fail. In this chapter, you will see how a flexible structure can provide further security.

However, before exploring this further, it is helpful to take the opposite view for a moment and recognize that there is a danger in playing too safe – you may never develop your business to its full potential. There are plenty of small businesses around who stay very small. Their owners rub along, making a living, but not growing or becoming really successful because they do not want to take any risks, or perhaps thay do not even think about what risks they could take.

The key feature of most well-known, successful businesses which started from nothing is that the founders took a great deal of risk – mortgaged their houses and raised plenty of funding – to single-mindedly pursue their idea. They worked day and night to get things off the ground, often losing partners along the way. After a number of setbacks, the gamble paid off and they made millions.

You may have no ambition to follow in their footsteps, sacrificing your personal life and risking losing everything. Yet it does not have to be all or nothing; there are risks that you may want to take to create a step change in your business and to move it from only ticking over to running very nicely. This is obviously a balancing act: much of this chapter is about caution, but there may be times when you are sure it is right to throw it to the wind! Flexibility in your business structure will help you to master this balancing act.

Contingency planning

The point of building flexibility into your business is to weather the many storms that you may face. The ones that occur most frequently are likely to be:

1 Economic recession.
2 Market change.
3 Bad debts.
4 Failure of supply.
5 Ruthless competition.
6 Running out of cash.

To address these problems, your business needs flexibility in its finance, its customer base, its market positioning, its route to market and its suppliers. Not many businesses set out with flexibility as an objective, but it almost invariably pays off to invest in it, and that investment may only involve your time.

Economic recession

Imagine, if a recession hits, what the impact will be on your business. If you are a business consultant specializing in cost savings, your business might improve. If you are selling home cinemas, you are likely to be hit hard. If you are selling luxury yachts, it may make no difference – the rich stay rich, even in a recession.

If you were in the home cinema market, how could you acquire more flexibility in case of recession? Selling to the very rich is one way to go, or selling other products which are more life essentials than a cinema. Increasing your sales and marketing activity is another option if you really are a one-product, one-market position company, but in that situation it would be hard to avoid taking a hit.

Market change

The most extreme examples of this phenomenon are fashions in children's toys and games. The Barbie doll, the skateboard, cabbage patch dolls, pet rocks – all these things become crazes, and then another fad replaces them and you can be left with a warehouse full of yesterday's favourite. The same thing happens in most markets, but not so visibly. It is often a serious problem because, unlike hula-hoops, the decline can be hard to detect and by the time you have noticed it, you are probably suffering badly.

The obvious solution is to watch the market closely and look for new trends to follow. If you were making typewriters, you would have had a big job moving into computers. However, perhaps there was a halfway point, in keyboard manufacture, for example, or maybe your manufacturing facilities were appropriate for other related industrial products such as machine controls. Flexibility was vital to avoid extinction in the typewriter market, but most cases are not so extreme, especially if you pick up the trend early enough.

Bad debt

The story of bad debt is the same for many small companies. A large client, who they have dealt with in the past, places a big order and then does not pay for perhaps 90 days, or perhaps never. The route through the courts is expensive and will take too long, so either they are flexible enough to take the hit or they go under.

Money in the bank is always useful at times like this, but so is the ability to take extended credit from your suppliers, and to get an overdraft or a loan from the bank without having to spend a year writing business plans.

Failure of supply

This is a less common problem, but if the only supplier you know of dinky nodules goes bust, and these just happen to be a key component in your product, you may be in trouble. Back-up sources are always a good tool to have in your flexible kit bag.

Ruthless competition

The supermarkets versus the corner shops springs to mind as an example here, but corner shops are usually selling convenience, not price. A better example is the Internet, where consumers search for the cheapest washing machine online, and then go to you, their local electrical store, and ask you to match it. You cannot, because you have all the overheads of a shop, not just a website, and you cannot buy in the same volume to get the lower price.

You may have to reduce your price, but you are unlikely to be able to match it. You will, of course, sell service, information, immediate delivery, a friendly local face, and quiz them about the online extras – did the price include VAT and delivery? Was it exactly the same model? Indeed, have they considered any other model? The bottom line is that you will almost certainly have to take a margin hit, not to match the Internet, but to come close enough to justify all those additional benefits you offer.

Running out of cash

This is often a consequence of all of the above factors, but particularly bad debts, combined with a failure to build the right relationships with your suppliers and your bank, who may not be very understanding when you desperately need their help.

The above examples show the need for flexibility, and the form that flexibility might need to take. The next section examines some key factors in building flexibility into your business.

Financial flexibility

Figure 7 shows a model of a financially flexible business. You see very low overheads, moderate direct costs, delivering a nice, fat profit margin, delivering a very healthy profit margin. The fixed costs are so low that there is minimal regular outlay on rent, salaries, etc., and most of the cost varies according to sales volume, making the business very flexible because it needs little revenue to support its fixed costs. This could be a mail order business selling toys, which is run from home. Figure 7 cannot show stock levels, but our mail order business promises delivery in 14 days and generally has time to order stock in small batches, often to match orders received. This makes them far more flexible.

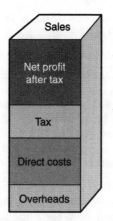

Figure 7 Financially flexible business

If the same business were run as a shop, with two part-time assistants, the fixed costs would immediately go up, and of course there would be more stock for display purposes and so the business becomes less flexible.

The message here is not to close down your shop and open a mail order business. Children are much more likely to buy, or ask their parents to buy, if the toy is right in front of them and consequently there are benefits to having a good display.

Children also want their toy right now, and having the goods in stock will stop the parents going elsewhere, even if they could find it cheaper at a superstore – you have it available here and now, you have the edge.

Accepting then, that a shop is a good route to market, it will almost always have higher fixed costs than an Internet business. Recognize this and maximize the flexibility within those boundaries, or look for the flexibility elsewhere – in the management and control of stock, or through negotiating better credit terms with your suppliers, for example.

The other key factors in the financial arena to give flexibility in business are obtaining better payment terms from your clients, better prices from your suppliers, good credit control, minimizing business debt and having tight cash management. All of these are covered in Chapter 13.

Market flexibility

Flexibility in the market boils down to two things:

1 Having a variety of product or service offerings.
2 Increasing your sales through broader market coverage.

By broadening your market coverage, either through different markets or different routes to market, and by offering a variety of products or services, you will also be building a bigger and more varied customer base, which provides more stability than a narrow homogenous group. This will enable you to cope much better with an economic recession, as well as with any decline in a specific market. Here are the obvious permutations:

1 Same product offered to different market(s).
2 Different product(s) offered to same market.
3 Variation on the product in the same market.
4 Variation on the product in a different market.
5 Different product(s) offered to different markets.

For products also read services, and go very carefully with the last option 5, which looks like a business start-up in a new field, and should be approached accordingly. It is much better to have at least one foot on familiar ground.

Markets can be categorized in different ways:

• By price point: low, medium, high.
• By purchaser: retail, trade or business.

- By activity or sector: sports, engineering, fashion.
- By application: finished goods or components.

Case study

Toby's scented candle making is an example of a business with good market spread. Toby makes candles in the medium price point range; he does not do 'cheap and nasty', and he thinks he has no access to the luxury market. He sells to the trade in England through a small chain of gift shops in the Midlands, to a group of aromatherapists in Birmingham, and to a few local florists. He sells to retail consumers via his website, and to business by visiting large companies in the area in November and offering special Christmas decorations featuring his candles for their reception areas. His market sectors are home decor, business decor, and personal health and well-being. Toby mostly provides finished goods, but to the florists he is effectively providing components.

If one market goes into decline, Toby has plenty of others to focus on, and indeed he has not exhausted all the market opportunities yet. His view of the luxury market needs challenging, for example. It is clear that Toby is very flexible in his approach to different markets, and he has even diversified a little by offering his products combined with others in the business sector. The seasonality of this offering is well balanced by his other market outlets, particularly the aromatherapists, who are unlikely to vary their purchasing pattern very much over the year.

Routes to market – retail

1 Shop.
2 Market stall.
3 Partner with other shops who act as distributors or agents.
4 Craft fairs/exhibitions.
5 Mail order catalogue.
6 Website.
7 eBay

Toby also has a good spread of routes to market. In addition to using shops as sales agents and his website, he sells direct to business customers and attends some major craft fairs for the trade, and one or two big local fairs for retail customers.

Routes to market – trade or business

1 Selling direct.
2 Factory counter sales.
3 Distributor/reseller.
4 Exhibitions.
5 Mail order.
6 Website.
7 eBay

If you make widgets for the motor trade, you may feel that your market and your route to market are pretty fixed, but it is helpful to follow Toby's model for a moment. Having a widget website might attract overseas customers, especially if it is a specialized product. If you sell to the big boys, what about all the small ones – the restorers of old cars, for example? Could you diversify to make replica vintage widgets? This would provide a much better margin, much easier people to deal with, and an easy market to find on the Internet – just type in 'vintage Jaguar restorers' and press Go! When Ford or Honda decide they do not like your widgets, how satisfying would it be to have built up a significant percentage of your sales outside your home country, or from small specialized restorers?

This strategy will also make you less vulnerable to ruthless competitors, who almost invariably operate in larger marketplaces. If you also have an established niche, you are unlikely to encounter any aggressive competitive activity there. Of course there will be competitors, but in a niche which tends to be a smaller community, the competition tends to focus on quality and service levels.

In summary, it is safe to say that a flexible business is a well-run business. However, there is one caveat, some aspects of financial flexibility are about minimizing risk, and there are times to take risks in business if you want to grow or make significant changes.

Flexibility means that your business is more stable, and more able to cope with any problems that arise, particularly those outside your control such as a client going bankrupt. You achieve flexibility by applying as many of the following flexibility factors as you can:

• Low fixed costs
• Low or no financing costs
• Excellent payment terms from your clients

- Good credit terms from your suppliers
- Wide profit margin
- Rapid stock turnover (if you have stock)
- Maximum tax avoidance
- A good number of varied clients
- Sales to different markets
- Sales via different routes to market
- Best deals from your suppliers
- A back-up source of finance in place (ideally also some cash reserves).

Given this broad-based profile for your company, you will be set to weather storms and also to build an even more successful business.

Steps to success

Key questions to ask:

1 What is my attitude to risk?
2 Am I holding the company back, or extending it too far?
3 How would I cope in an economic crisis?
4 Is my customer base broad enough to give me stability in hard times?
5 If not, how could I broaden it?
6 How well do I score on the flexibility factors?

20

good business relationships

In this chapter you will learn:

- the benefits of good relationships
- how to select your contacts
- the definition of a good relationship
- how to build different business relationships.

The need to build good business relationships seems fairly obvious, you may be thinking, and indeed it is. However, we do not always do the obvious, although we intend to, and a key reason for this is that we may not see the benefits clearly.

The benefits of good relationships

So why bother to build good relationships? To answer this, here is a list of the benefits that good business relationships will bring to your business:

- Sales leads
- Referrals and recommendations
- Enhanced reputation
- Market intelligence
- Business information
- Support
- Advice
- Loyalty
- Contacts
- Help in a crisis.

Case study

Contrast two manufacturers of small metal components, both about the same size, both running a successful operation. Raj cultivates relationships, Robin does not. Suddenly their major client goes into receivership, and cannot pay its suppliers. Raj, who has built a very close spirit of teamwork with his main suppliers, agrees extended terms with them and, with some help from the bank which also knows him well, he survives the crisis. Robin attempts to do what Raj does but, as he has no solid foundation on which to ask for help, he gets very little co-operation and, after struggling for a while, his business folds.

Robin does not think that this was his fault – what happened to his key client was totally outside his control, and he treated his suppliers well, paying promptly and having a good businesslike relationship, as he did with the bank. In fact, he had little reason to talk to any of these people, and only did so when a specific issue arose.

Unlike Robin, Raj is annoyed with himself for not seeing the client problem coming. He resolves to get closer to his clients, and keep his ear to the ground for this kind of information. He also recognizes that he should not have had so many eggs in one client basket, which this crisis has forced him to address.

If you asked them, Robin would tell you he had good working relationships, and Raj would tell you some of his were good, but some were not good enough. You can assess the validity of their comments from the state of their respective businesses, which is crystal clear in this case, but you do not want to risk a complete business collapse in order to check on the quality of your own business relationships.

Selecting your contacts

Before we go any further, let us examine who exactly we could be building relationships with. People who work for us are top of the list, but this is so important that it is dealt with separately in Chapter 18, and will not be included here. You should be building relationships with the following:

- Clients
- Suppliers
- Investors
- Banks
- Colleagues (in other non-competing businesses)
- Competitors
- Institutions, associations and local business groups
- Press and media
- Community.

If you have many clients and suppliers plus a few investors, this may look like a very long list. Before we consider it further, let us define what we mean by a good business relationship.

The definition of a good relationship

The amount you invest in a relationship should be roughly proportional to the amount you expect to get from it. You will therefore put more energy into clients and less into institutions, but there are no hard and fast rules. If you have a handful of clients, you will obviously work much harder at each one than if you have hundreds of customers who buy from you every year or two. However, knowing your customer is one of the fundamental rules of business, so it will still be your priority.

Clients, suppliers, investors and the bank all require planned and consistent personal time investment. You have more choice about what to invest in colleagues, competitors and institutions, and you may not wish to invest at all in the press or the local community, depending on the nature of your operation.

If at this point you start to think 'I do it anyway' or 'I don't need all those people', think of Robin and then make a list of your target contacts or draw a mind map, with your business in the middle and all the contacts radiating out with their contacts beyond, so that you can see their potential value.

Now you will need to work out what it will take, in each case, to build a good working relationship, which at its strongest is well defined by Raj as one in which the supplier, bank or investor is prepared to trust and support you financially in a crisis. The essential elements of that good relationship are:

1 Punctual and reliable business transactions.
2 Regular communication and advance warning of any variation from the norm.
3 A personal interest in them as people, and in their businesses.

The results of building these three elements will be that you are seen as:

- **Reliable** – you deliver
- **Trustworthy** – you tell them if something goes awry
- **Open** – you let them know what is happening
- **Visible** – you keep in touch
- **Likeable** – you are interested in them.

This definition of a business relationship applies to all types of contact. A large variable element will be the individual you are dealing with, and this particularly applies to the personal side. Some people need to talk about the weather and their wife's bad back before they get down to business. Some people want to get straight on with the task in hand, and may not respond well to being asked about their holiday plans, but will usually be happy to discuss some aspect of their own business, perhaps when your business is satisfactorily concluded. Check this carefully and respond accordingly because it is a key aspect of establishing a really good business relationship.

In addition to the three core elements listed above, it is critical to know what it is that you want from each type of contact. If you think about this, it will usually be far more than the basic purpose of your phone call or visit.

How to build different relationships

Clients

Your client is Tom, from ABC Plc. Test the quality of your relationship as a supplier to Tom and his company with the following questions:

Note: If you only sell to individuals, you can ignore the company questions.

- What does Tom want? (in the context of what you supply to him)
- What does his company want?
- What will Tom want in the future?
- What will his company want in the future?
- How does your product/service fit with Tom's current plans?
- What are Tom's future plans (personal/business)?
- How is Tom's company doing?
- What does Tom think of: you,
  your product/service
  your organization?

- Does Tom make purchasing decisions alone?
- If not, who is the real decision maker?
- Have you met him/her?
- Do you know anyone else in the company apart from Tom?
- Would Tom be willing to recommend you to someone else in his company?
- Would Tom be willing to recommend you to a new prospect?
- Does Tom have other contacts or suggestions for prospects for you to target?
- Would Tom be willing to act as your reference, to show or tell others how pleased he is with your product or service?
- Do you know something about Tom's personal life, his family, hobbies, career aims?

If you can answer all these questions, and have consistently met or exceeded Tom's expectations, you can congratulate yourself on having a good client relationship. If Tom is one of hundreds of clients, you cannot possibly gather all that data but you will want to gather data on Tom as a category of client, and learn as much about a 'typical Tom' as you can.

In summary, you want to know how well you are meeting his current needs, what you need to do to meet his future needs, whether he can provide any leads, and whether he will still be around to keep paying you.

Suppliers

It can be tempting to treat suppliers as second-class citizens, but treating them well pays off, as Raj in the case study could tell you. Evidently, they will vary enormously in importance to your business – for Raj, they were key to his manufacturing operation.

If Raj had been a marketing consultant, suppliers would most likely be his accountant or the man who looks after his computer equipment – not fundamental to the business at all – but Raj will still get a better service out of suppliers that like and trust him, that he pays on time, and that he treats with respect. This means that he will have shown an interest in them personally, and in their business, and invested time in talking to them about them, and not just about the problem with VAT or the computer. It may be that they could provide Raj with leads, or useful contacts. They will certainly be far more patient creditors if he hits a cash flow problem and has to delay paying them for a while. He might get better terms from them too. In summary, suppliers can deliver better terms, extended credit, better service, leads, contacts and useful information.

Investors

If you have investors in your business, you are likely to have set up a regular communication plan with them in some form. They may attend monthly meetings or you may send them regular financial reports. If by any chance you have not done this, do so because the essence of good investor relations is reliability. You have committed to deliver to them, and therefore you will tell them regularly how you are doing and in advance if anything deviates from what they are expecting. They need reassurance that you are in control, even if you are not on track, and consequently good communication is fundamental.

Investors can also give you many other things and, when you meet them, it is worth exploring what they have to offer, as well as giving them your business data. They are likely to have business experience and knowledge, good business contacts, leads and market intelligence. Make the most of what they have to give (Chapter 26 on funding covers the relationship more fully).

Banks

There was a time when you could take your bank manager out
to lunch or they might take you out, but they are harder to find
these days, guarded by business advisers and call centres. It is still
important to have a relationship with the person you would be
dealing with if you needed help in a crisis. You may know only
too well who that is, or you may be like Joe, who runs a very
successful Web design service from his spare room, and has never
needed anything from the bank other than a business account.

Whatever your circumstances, it is worth building a relationship
with this key bank contact, who we will call your bank manager
for the sake of convenience. First make sure that you are dealing
with the right person, and not a minion. If in doubt, ask who
you would speak to if you wanted a business loan in six figures,
or whatever number makes sense for your organization.

When you know who they are, arrange to meet them – lunch is
probably overkill these days. The best time to do this is when
business is good and you do not want a thing from them. You
can then build the relationship, and talk about how they can
help you in the future, financially and with advice and guidance.
After that, arrange to keep in touch at whatever interval seems
appropriate, but at least annually.

If you are like Joe, and are determined never to borrow a penny
from a bank, it is still worth building the relationship, as he
discovered. After two years' trading, his account was always
heavily in the black, and on his second meeting with his bank
manager, he managed to negotiate a reduction in his bank
charges! Even though Joe feels rock solid financially, he is still
wise to keep up the relationship. He may come across a
wonderful opportunity that needs some instant funding, and he
is much more likely to get it if he has managed the bank
relationship well.

Colleagues

You may be tempted to think of people you know in business as
just people you know, but it is worth reconsidering the list of
benefits again, because you can get all of them from colleagues.
Not all from the same one perhaps, but from a variety of sources.

You may have one or two colleagues who qualify as business
buddies, and these are invaluable. Building up a network of
other contacts can be a worthwhile investment. Where and how

you do this depends on the nature of your business. If the local area is important to you, as it will be if you run a shop, for example, building up contacts via your local chamber of commerce or one of the business contact groups will be worthwhile. It will be really important to you to know what is going on in your area, and to raise your profile there, as well as gathering local intelligence. Fellow shopkeepers can always help each other out in practical ways too.

If, like Joe, you run a business over the Internet, your local area will be far less important. You are more likely to form a network of people who do similar but not identical work to your own. If your skills are complementary, you have the opportunity to cross-refer work, as you would if you did similar work but in different market sectors, and you can also share problems and ideas.

Competitors

People generally fall into two camps when dealing with competitors. Either they avoid them or they cultivate them, and generally people who do the latter come off best.

If you are a consultant of any kind, cultivating your competitors can pay dividends because they have limited resources and need external help to cope with overload. Nigel Wyatt who runs Magenta Circle (www.magentacircle.co.uk), a networking organization for consultants, observed, 'I get far more business from my competitors than anyone else. For a start they are the only people who truly understand what I do. They often run out of resources, and they know they can trust me not to steal their clients.' This is far less likely to be the case if you have a product to sell, but it does happen that factories run out of capacity or stock and, if they know you as a friendly face, they may turn to you for supply to cover themselves in an emergency, and you might have a similar need of them.

In building this relationship, it is important to be up front about your competitive status, and say that although you compete, there may be times when you can help each other out, and that you want to put your relationship on a friendly footing. You may find that you are not as competitive as you thought, that they operate in different areas or at different price levels. You may have useful information to share about suppliers or even clients. Much can come from studying the competition. If you are able to do it first hand, so much the better.

Institutions, associations and local business groups

Your key objective here is to find out what such bodies have to offer you in the way of advice, information, leads and contacts. If you belong to a professional body, be sure you know what you receive for that annual subscription. It may be much more than you think.

Conversely, if you are considering joining an association, such as the Institute of Directors or the local chamber of commerce, check on what exactly you will be getting, and what you have to pay extra for. The use of a smart London address might be far less important to you than joining a ready-made local network.

Whatever you decide, make the most of it. If it is the chamber of commerce, find out who is who in your local area and who might be useful to know bearing in mind the factory extension you are planning or the change to your shop front. If it is just your professional body to give you access to the library service, it is still worth getting to know Rose, who handles all the requests and is so keen on the theatre.

Press and media

'What has the press and media got to do with me?', might be your first question, thinking of the likelihood of your business featuring on the front page of the *Financial Times*. However, with small businesses we are usually thinking of specialized or local media.

Case study

Dennis advertises his restoration business regularly in the Jaguar Motor Club magazine. He knows the editor, the photographer and the advertising manager really well and, as club member himself, he has won a prize or two. Because they see him as a 'good bloke', and a good club member, they are happy to include him in their articles, whereas other restorers might be viewed only as trade and restricted to placing advertisements. Clients are impressed to find that Dennis is an enthusiast like themselves, and not just a mechanic or garage owner. Dennis is lucky to have a magazine aimed totally at his target audience. If you can find one, it is certainly worth some effort on your part, and not just advertising money.

If you operate locally, you may want to consider doing something to attract news coverage from your local radio, newspaper or TV station. Think of an idea, and then find the right person to talk to and ask them about it:

'I'm thinking of sponsoring a mini marathon for children in fancy dress for the paediatric ward of the local hospital. Would that be of interest to your publication?'

If they say no, this is still an opportunity for relationship building, so you can ask what would interest them, how to get good coverage, when to hold the event, etc. Even if nothing comes of it this time, you now have a useful contact in the local media.

Community

Communities can exist in many forms – you might belong to a community of eBay buyers and sellers of teddy bears; a national community of yoga instructors; or just your local village, suburb or city community.

In all cases, you are concerned with your reputation in that community. In the case of eBay, you are dealing with clients, prospects and suppliers. Therefore, all the rules of relationship building apply, even though the contact is by e-mail or telephone.

In the case of yoga, you are dealing with colleagues, competitors and possibly associates. The effort you put in here will depend on the size and quality of your existing network, your potential need for associates or associate work, and whether you are aiming to target this audience as clients, to teach the teachers.

In the case of the local area, you are dealing with clients, prospects and the whole spectrum of other contacts, including potential future staff.

Case study

It is easy to underestimate the impact your reputation can have locally, and this is very well illustrated by Henry Stewart, of Happy Computers. Henry gives his staff time off to do charitable work. Happy has about 50 staff, and they are free to do whatever work interests them, from helping the starving in Africa through to teaching the elderly how to use a computer, providing they can show benefit to the community and to the business. Often the business benefit is from the training and development of Happy's staff; they face new challenges and gain valuable experience while working for good causes.

The effect on the business is clearly measurable. Henry has a huge waiting list (currently over 2000) of people who want to join the company. His staff turnover is half the national average for his industry since his staff do not want to leave, and his company has a shining reputation for delivering excellent service. There is an immediate assumption that people in a company which gives so much to charity must be good at what they do, which is quickly confirmed by the actual experience – his staff are excellent and so enthusiastic about their work. This also leads to the strongest customer loyalty.

Happy Computers has had lots of media coverage, not just locally, but at national level. This is worth far more than any amount of advertising spend, and Happy Computers is financially successful as a result. This is the perfect illustration of the virtuous circle – good business relationships translate into a good bottom line.

Steps to success

Key questions to ask:

1 What benefits do I see in good business relationships?
2 How many of the following are relevant to my business?
   - Clients
   - Suppliers
   - Investors
   - Banks
   - Colleagues (in other non-competing businesses)
   - Competitors
   - Institutions, associations and local business groups
   - Press and media
   - Community.
3 Of those that are relevant from the above list, how many deliver benefits to my business?
4 What could I do to improve on the benefits from business relationships?
5 How systematic and effective is my approach to each group in question 2?
6 Which relationship(s) could have the biggest impact on my business?

21

a clear focus

You started your business with a clear aim in mind, but over time you have become absorbed in the day-to-day running of the operation, and somehow lost sight of your original goal. The effects of this can be great: you may be trying to do too many things outside your specialist area, and you may not feel that you are doing them as well as you would like, or you may not enjoy doing them, or both.

Checking on your focus level

Focus diverted

Case study

Dennis loved cars, but his particular passion was old Jaguars. After working for a number of car repair companies, he set up his own restoration business in his garage, specializing in vintage Jaguars. He was well known in the car club, advertised in the club magazine, and soon had more business than he could cope with. He hired a few people, choosing carefully, moved to bigger premises and things went well for a while, then he hit a lull, and took in some work on modern cars. This work multiplied, and then someone asked if he would sell a car for him and, before he knew it, he was running an operation far distant from his beginnings, or rather it was running him. He was doing nothing but work, and when he began to see signs of a recession coming, he decided to take stock of his operation. Neither he nor his team really enjoyed the work on the modern cars, and selling second-hand cars was just a nuisance.

Dennis had lost focus on what his business is about. He just took any market opportunity that came along, because naturally one does not want to miss an opportunity, but in fact having done some growing, Dennis has discovered that growth is not his primary aim! He really wants to enjoy what he does and, as long as he makes a good living out of that, he does not want to do anything other than restore vintage Jaguars and he has recruited a team who feel the same way. Although he is prepared to devote the majority of his time to the business, Dennis would also like some free time to remind his wife and children what he looks like.

Dennis regained his focus by diverting from it and discovering what his priorities were in the process. Armed with this knowledge, you might be able to take a short cut. Ask the following questions:

- What was the business I set out to run?
- What business am I in now?
- Is that the business I feel passionate about?
- What do I want from my business?

Answers to the last question could be anything from 'personal fulfilment' to 'To sell it in ten years' time and make a few million'.

When you are clear on what business you are in, whether it is the one you want to be in, and what you want from it, then you can work on clarifying your focus.

Rediscovering your focus

You may have the opposite problem to Dennis. You may be like Jack, who wanted to restore vintage cars but never made it past the modern ones. He knows only too well that he is not in the business he originally aimed for, but for some reason he cannot get there. He may have fallen for the low hanging fruit on the tree – business that was easy to get. This kept him busy, and meant that he did not put any real effort into his original goal.

The key question is – how does Jack feel about that? If the answer is not too worried because he is making money, then he can redefine his goal. Jack's aim is not to restore vintage cars – that is what Dennis wants. Jack's aim is to make money out of repairing cars. As soon as he redefines his goal, it immediately enables him to tighten his focus. The next question is to ask how Jack can make more money out of repairing cars. If he could make a great deal more from vintage cars, this is an option to pursue, but perhaps he could make more money by qualifying as a registered repair centre. Jack can now plan for the future without hanging on to the vague idea that he 'should' be in the vintage market.

Defining your outcome

If you have lost focus because you never really were clear about your aims in the first place, then, like Jack, you are going to achieve a great deal once you are clear about your goal. The answers may not come so easily, and you may need to test your thinking more rigorously. Start by writing down your possible goals or outcomes in positive terms, for example:

- To gain a reputation for excellence in restoring vintage Jaguars.
- To build a successful car repair business.

Jot down as many as you can think of. It goes without saying that you are in business to make money and there is no need to put that in every option unless you feel passionately that you need to.

Creating a clear outcome

When you have formed a view of each outcome, try going there. Create a really clear picture in your mind, step inside it and see what happens. If you have difficulty creating mental pictures, and some people do, perhaps an impression with feelings and sounds would work for you.

Imagine restoring really interesting cars – what will that be like? This is a good way of evaluating each option, by imagining that it has already happened, and finding out what it feels, looks and sounds like. If it feels right, put it on your positive list, if not, double-check and then reject it. You may find that you are missing some information. If the option looks promising, investigate, and then go back and try it out. When you have found the option which works best for you, test it thoroughly with these questions:

- Why is achieving this outcome important to me?
- How will I measure success?
- What will I see, hear and feel when I achieve this outcome? (Really imagine achieving this outcome with lots of detail.)
- What is the context in which this outcome will be achieved? (When, where, who with, etc.)

Now you have a clear view of what you want, the next stage is to test it against other things. Firstly, the effect on the rest of your life. Will it mean no holidays, working weekends or not seeing your family? Weigh these things against what you want to see if it is worth the sacrifice:

- How does this fit?
- What will be the effect on the balance of the rest of my life and on others?
- Is this acceptable to me and is it representative of who I am or who I want to be?

Next, consider the problems you may hit:

- What barriers might I face?

- How will I get over these barriers?
- What are the things that hold me back at present?
- What stops me?

'It is easy to stay as I am.' This is often the reaction of someone who does not want to change and, for some, the rewards are not big enough to push them into action. If you are feeling this way, ask yourself the following questions:

- How is my present situation useful to me?
- Is the reward of achieving this outcome big enough to compensate for the loss of how things are now?
- If not, what would it take for the new outcome to be really compelling?

You know you will probably need some external resources to get what you want, but more important at this stage is to identify what personal resources you will need to call upon to make the change happen. Perhaps those qualities of initiative, determination and enthusiasm which enabled you to start off the business in the first place are appropriate. Whatever the personal resources are, recalling how they worked for you in the past will enable you to call upon them now.

- What are the internal resources I need to achieve my outcome?
- What are the three or four most important resources? Recall when you have had these in the past.

Finally, two last steps. First, a double-check on whether you do really want to do this, and whether you could make it even more attractive. Second, a check that you are actually going to make a start:

- Desirability check. Do I really want this?
- What else could I add to this plan to make it more desirable?
- What is my first step?
- What specifically will I do?
- What is the action I will commit to?

Imagine yourself taking the first step.

If you are happy with the answers to all these questions, you have a well-formed outcome and, with it, the clarity of focus which will deliver success. If you find difficulty, particularly in balancing the rewards of change against staying as you are, work on those issues.

Find an outcome that delivers greater rewards than those you get from staying as you are. It may be that you do not change the outcome at all; you focus on existing rewards, enhance them, find more of them, or see more disadvantages in not changing. However you do it, the end result will clear your path to success, and remove any nagging doubts from the back of your mind so that you can just go for it!

Focus unattainable?

If you started on course, but you have simply taken a wrong turning and need to get back on track, like Dennis, your way forward is clear. However, if you have lost focus because you found that what you originally intended was not possible, that is a different problem entirely. If your market has disappeared, for example, there is little point in keeping the same focus and you need to move your business in a different direction. Nonetheless, it may be that you have not been single-minded enough in your focus.

Case study

Let us go back to Jack. This time he tells us that he really does want to work with vintage cars and he finds the modern ones unrewarding, but he just cannot get the business. That may be because Dennis is round the corner, or there may be many other explanations. What is certain is that keeping the business going with modern vehicles is a distraction from the original goal. It may be keeping body and soul together, but if it did not exist, Jack would be trying for vintage business a great deal harder than he is now.

Having accepted that Jack and his staff have to live, and that the 'distraction' must continue to pay the mortgages, there is still a great deal that Jack can do to reach his goal. First, he must disconnect as far as possible from the day-to-day operation so that he can focus all his attention on winning vintage business. The first thing he will do is define his outcome clearly, using the process described in the section above, making it financially realistic and attainable. Ideally, he will involve his team in some way, either in creating the outcome, or in sharing it with them and asking for their input.

Jack and his team come up with the following: 'In 12 months' time, a third of our business (at current revenue level) will be vintage repairs.' Jack writes this down on a whiteboard on the office wall. Research shows that you are 25 per cent more likely to achieve a goal if you have written it down, and the percentage increases again if you share your goal with others.

Jack holds a meeting with his team to come up with business ideas, and he formulates a plan, with dates for activities. He decides that talking to Dennis might be instructive, and he wants to be sure that their business is complementary and not competitive. Little does he know that Dennis will offer to do a deal to transfer his modern repair work to Jack, but that is another story!

Moving forward

When you have your focus, and turn it into a goal that you record and share with others, you can plan to achieve it. Be ruthless about meeting that plan – do not allow yourself to be lured back into the day-to-day pattern that will keep you where you are – and not where you want to be.

If your plan does not work, and you are not getting the business that you are aiming for, it is time to take stock. Perhaps some advice about sales or marketing or both is needed (see Chapter 17). The key is to know where you want to go, and then it is not difficult to work out that you are not getting there. Here are a couple of quotations to illustrate the point:

'Our plans miscarry because they have no aim. When a man does not know what harbour he is making for, no wind is the right wind.'

Seneca, 3 BC–AD 65

'The trouble with not having a goal is that you can spend your life running up and down the field and never score.'

Bill Copeland

No focus

Perhaps the most difficult problem to deal with is when you are not really sure what you want, and then the problem of focus becomes secondary. The key question is what do you want to focus on? If you do not know the answer, you are likely to spread yourself too thinly, which often means that you will lose business.

Case study

Mary started out as a business consultant, advising on project plans. Soon she was asked to run training courses on project management, and then she agreed to manage a project which involved restructuring a telesales operation. This was quickly followed by another, for a sister company. Now she has been asked to work on a plan for a new call centre, and she is feeling uncomfortable because she is not an expert in this area. When she takes stock of where she is, she realizes that she has let her clients lead her in many different directions, and now she is not sure where she wants to go.

This is a case where Mary needs to understand what she wants from her business, and to do this she can employ the technique of stepping into the future, and see what it would be like to follow up her various options. She makes a list of these, not just the things she has done already, but also the things that she would like to do. She steps into each option, and imagines what it will be like. She does not simply think about it quickly; she really goes there in her head, working out what she will see, hear and feel when she performs each role. She logs each one, and comes up with a rating, although in one or two cases she is sure that this is a clear yes or no.

Mary's conclusion is that she does not want to run projects. This takes her into areas outside her expertise and makes her uncomfortable. She will turn down the latest piece of business she has been offered and focus on what she really wants to do, which is to help others manage projects. This is an excellent test of her commitment: if she is happy to turn down business that does not match her focus it means that she is really clear about what she wants and what she does not want.

Reinforcing focus: your elevator statement

If you have clarity of focus, you can use it to write your elevator statement, which will reinforce the focus even more. An elevator statement has little to do with lifts, but it has this name because it illustrates the ability to tell someone what you do quickly and simply. If you were to get in a lift with a key prospect who did not know anything about you, your elevator statement would cover it in the time it takes to get to the third floor, which is not long!

Another way to think of it is when you meet someone at a party and they ask what you do. You may not be looking to win business at a party, but contacts are contacts, and it is useful to have a neat and tidy description that encapsulates what you do: 'I make and sell decorative candles' or 'I offer specialist tax advice to small businesses' both tell a great deal in a short space of time.

This may seem obvious, but in fact many people cannot tell you what they do in brief. First impressions count here, and it is important to remember that people like to pigeon hole you, so give them something quick and simple to grasp. People are also unlikely to ask you for clarification and when you say, 'I'm in business development' they are unlikely to enquire, 'What does that mean, exactly?' They will have their own view of business development and fit you into their preconception, which is fine if they think of you with superb marketing and commercial skills, but if they have an idea it is something to do with building industrial estates, that may not be the pigeon hole you want to be slotted into. It is therefore vital that your statement is clear and easy to understand.

Case study
Mary spends some time thinking about how she will describe herself. She eventually settles on: 'I help project managers to become outstanding managers of projects.' She will try this out on a few friends, to make sure the words roll off the tongue easily, but she is happy that it reflects exactly what she wants to do. As she says the words, she feels focused, and sounds confident and enthusiastic. Now that she has written her statement, she starts to think of people she might talk to, and things she could do to develop the business in that direction. She will test her statement by watching carefully for people's responses to what she says. She will look for the flicker of interest or the glazed expression, and the more abstract the description, the more likely she is to get the glazing over.

If she had chosen the words: 'Consulting in project management processes and techniques', for example, that description would be harder to grasp because it is more vague and general. The more general the statement is, the less likely people are to ask about it. The words will also have an impact on you, too, because it is much easier to focus on something specific and concrete, rather than something abstract and general.

Here are some guidelines for writing your statement:

1 Avoid abstract words – they tend to be slippery in two ways:
   - First, they allow the listener to slide over them without fully registering their meaning.
   - Second and worse, they are hard to pin down, and people will not ask.
2 Include a clear business benefit relevant to the prospect
   - 'I provide tax advice to small businesses.'
   - 'We install rental gymnasium equipment into companies who care about staff fitness.'
3 Be clear about your specialism, if you have one. Someone who 'provides tax advice to small businesses' will be more appealing to a small business prospect than someone who generally 'provides business tax advice'.
4 Keep it personal – use 'I' or 'we'.
5 Keep it active, not passive. Do not say 'Our service is designed to deliver…', but 'We deliver…'.

If you do not have a good elevator statement, now is the best time to write one. Test it out on friends or colleagues, and look for the light of understanding in their eyes as you say it. Give it some careful thought because it is not really an exercise in choosing your words carefully, it is about the fundamental purpose of your business. When you have focus, your way ahead becomes clear. Even when there are obstacles on that road, they are less of a barrier because you have a clear direction. Henry Ford (1863–1947) put it like this: 'Obstacles are those frightful things you see when you take your eyes off your goals.'

With your eyes on your goals, it is also much easier to make a plan to reach them. The plan will be realistic but challenging and, above all, achievable. When you have real clarity of business focus, that clarity will translate directly into business success.

Steps to success

Key questions to ask:

1 How would I describe the focus of my business?
2 Do I still have the same business focus that I started with?
3 If it has changed, how do I feel about the change?
4 If it has changed, how have I redefined it?
5 If I am unclear, can the outcome model help me?
6 Can I describe my business clearly in a single sentence?

22 commitment to business success

In this chapter you will learn:
- to check on your passion and focus
- about commitment to goals, not activities
- about coping with failure
- proactive perseverance
- to prioritize.

You may have been lucky enough to start your business easily, and found that it just worked. Now you have hit a plateau, or worse, a decline, and you are asking yourself why. You now wonder if it is all worth the effort, especially as it was all so easy at the beginning.

Or you may have had the opposite experience of pushing water uphill to get your business going, and even now it still needs huge amounts of effort, and you too are questioning whether you want to go on in this way.

The real test of a business is when it has been going for a while and now it falters. Can you make it fly, or will it drag you down? In most cases it will be your actions that determine the future. There may be external factors influencing your market or your cash flow, but 99 times out of 100 it is down to you. You will need to demonstrate real commitment, and be both proactive and persevering. With these qualities you are sure to succeed.

Checking passion and focus

You will already have your passion for the business and your focus on your goals. If your passion has faded or your focus has gone fuzzy, read Chapter 15 on passion or Chapter 21 on focus before you continue because these are the foundations we are about to build on. Without those our commitment plan is going to be shaky.

As a test, ensure that you can, right now, describe your passion for the business with feeling, and sum up your focus in a sentence or two. We'll take Ted as an example, who is a local newsagent: 'I have a passion for good local service as part of the community. I like people to come in here and feel that they are in the heart of the village. But having that passion does not seem to make ends meet. The shop makes enough to survive on, but it's long hours and I can't afford much help. So my focus is to sell more and to make more profit, but I've got quite a good customer base, and I can't charge any higher prices, so I'm thinking of packing it all in and buying a smallholding.'

Ted still has his passion, and his focus on increasing profits is very clear, but he is not achieving this goal and he is clearly losing commitment.

When we ask Ted about his focus he tells us: 'I know what I want, but I don't know how to get there. I've tried all the obvious things, so it's no good you telling me to persevere if I'm just going to do more of the same; it's getting me nowhere except older and more tired!'

Commitment to goals, not activities

Ted has put his finger on the key to this situation. Commitment does not mean simply keeping on doing the same things – that is commitment to activity; it means commitment to your goals, and this is a vital distinction. It is not enough to be persevering, it is critical to be proactive and persevering at the same time. Ted needs to think creatively about his business – if what he does is not working, he needs to do something else to achieve his goals.

'I do that – but it does me no good. It's all very well you suggesting that I talk to someone, but who would I talk to?' Ted needs a business buddy – ideally a newsagent in a distant and therefore non-competing area. His brother-in-law knows somebody who is very successful. They arrange to meet and swap ideas. Ted comes back full of enthusiasm: 'He majors on birthday cards – very good margin on those, apparently. And he specializes in old-fashioned sweets – in jars like they used to – puts a board outside the shop – that should go down really well here.' Ted's shop is in a pretty village with a great deal of tourist trade. He realizes that he had focused too much on the community, and not thought enough about the people coming to visit. Now he has something to get his teeth into. He makes a plan.

Ted starts with the cards, but finds they do not sell well. There is an excellent card shop a few doors along, and everyone goes there. He feels defeated, but then remembers 'proactive and persevering'. He goes to look at the competition, and decides to offer the old-fashioned type of card, with rhymes in, which are not at all the style of the card shop. Now he is no longer competing, the cards fit in better with his shop image, and sales start to pick up.

If you feel that you have been where Ted is a dozen times, and are now running out of steam, tell yourself that 'Success is a poor teacher'. In other words, you can learn a great deal from failure. A constructive way to look at things is to take the view that there is no such thing as failure, only feedback. Ted's initial failure with the greetings cards told him that he had a good competitor. He used this information to change his strategy, and now cards are part of his success story.

Coping with failure

Failure of any kind is always a blow and we often take it personally, which is human nature. Accept that you will probably be upset, annoyed or disappointed in some way, and give yourself time to recover from these feelings. Do not try to suppress or ignore them. When they have run their course, you will be ready to ask yourself the important question: what can I learn from this experience? Failure will always tell you something, but not to give up! If you use all the feedback it offers, you will be better equipped to try again.

Proactive perseverance

The essence of proactive perseverance is that you make a plan to achieve your business focus, and then stick to it. This plan will almost certainly mean doing something different. Generating ideas for something different will probably need some input from elsewhere or a complete rethink on your part to get out of a rut and come up with something new that will be effective. If some part of your plan fails, then this too is feedback to do something different.

It is important, in all this, to stay true to your passion and focus, and not just try many different things for the sake of doing something different. Ted's shop has not lost its community focus, and the new lines he has added fit perfectly with the profile of his local clients. You might add products or try different markets, but you are going somewhere else entirely if you do both at once. There is also the danger that if you change too many things at once, you do not get the opportunity to test each of the results, or you do not test things for long enough.

To support your commitment, it is really helpful to have a plan. Before your heart sinks, this can be the kind of plan that you can write on the back of an envelope over coffee, not a fancy business document.

Ted's plan

Ted spends little time on the target figures – just gives himself something to aim for. He works out that he needs to pay to carry more stock, but he has been cutting down on stock anyway lately, so he will not have a problem.

Focus – more profit.

Goals

- Sell £...... worth of greeting cards by year end.
- Sell £...... worth of sweets in jars by year end.
- Increase general sales to tourists by x% by year end.

Actions

Greetings cards:

- Investigate suppliers
- Check with buddy on rates to negotiate
- Full display by end March
- Do special window feature.

Old-fashioned sweets:

- Investigate suppliers
- Check with buddy on rates to negotiate
- Full display by end April
- Put advertising board outside

Review

Review sales at end September.

Have a meeting with buddy for more ideas in October.

If major spending had been involved, Ted might have wanted to do a more detailed financial plan to make sure that he could afford the stock, the display units, etc. In this case, he has all he needs and he thinks he has allowed enough time to really test the new lines. He has built in a review with his buddy to make sure that he is on track, and to start thinking about the next step, on the basis that if you are not moving forward you are probably moving backward.

Ted finds it stimulating to try new things, and he regains his enthusiasm. He gets into the habit of coming up with new angles. He starts to look at other newsagent's shops with a critical eye, looking for ideas. He chats to his customers more about the business: asks them what they think of the new lines, and if there is anything else they would like him to stock. He now has a new line in batteries, which was a popular request, and which he had thought another shop stocked, but his clients told him otherwise. The margin on batteries is good too, and he really feels he is getting somewhere, even though it is by slow small steps. The thought of that smallholding is no longer so appealing, in fact he thinks the grass here might be greener after all.

Ted's situation may look easy compared to yours, but the principles to apply are still the same:

1 Check that you are still passionate about your business.
2 Check that you are crystal clear about your focus.
3 Now ask what do I need to do differently to get there?
4 Make a plan to achieve your focus.
5 Set goals in the plan:
   • ...... date
   • £...... sales
   • ...... volume
   • £...... costs.

There is a saying that 'If you always do what you've always done, you will always get what you always got.' This is true of many things, including personal relationships. In business it may be more serious because, if you always do what you've always done, you may get far less than you used to as the market changes and you do not. Typewriters are the perfect illustration of this. If you had just carried on making them and ignored computers, your market would have evaporated completely.

Commitment does not mean just plodding on regardless. Do not mistake commitment to business activity for commitment to your goals; they are not the same but they are often confused. This is what can lead you down the typewriter road. In fact, it is often worse than the typewriter road because it is not so obvious that it is going nowhere – you just keep on and on until something makes you stop, or you run out of energy. To avoid falling into this trap, stay alert to any signs that your business is stalling or declining, and then start looking for the reasons.

You also need commitment to stick with something new in order to thoroughly test it out. Some people are butterflies rather than sticks in the mud. They are always trying new ideas, and then going on to the next one before they know if the first one really worked. There is a discipline here to do a proper job, and stay with it until you have evidence of its failure or success.

Prioritize

When you are clear on your new focus, perseverance and staying power are needed, but you should always be checking that you are still on the right road. All this may require some ruthless prioritizing on your part. It is so easy to fall into your regular 'daily doing routine', whatever that may be, and do the 'new stuff' later, 'when I've got this out of the way'. 'This' may be anything from a customer complaint to a VAT return, but it will not be the process of refocusing your business. Make this urgent, as well as important, and allocate a set time to do it every day.

Stay committed to your goals first, put your business activities second, and you will find the route to take your business where you want it to go.

Steps to success

Key questions to ask:

1 Do I regularly look for changes in my market, my business and myself?
2 How often do I review my business goals?
3 Do I have a written plan to achieve my goals?
4 How proactively do I pursue my goals?
5 Do I benchmark my business against similar companies?
6 How do I deal with failure?
7 How well do I evaluate the results of any changes I make?

part ³

moving on:

taking your business

to the next stage

23

defining success and creating vision

In this chapter you will learn:
- to define success
- what you want from your business
- how to create your vision.

This part of the book helps you to take your business on to the next level, whatever that may be. You may feel that you have reached a plateau and want to push beyond it. You may have expanded rapidly and feel uncomfortable. You may simply be unsure about where to go next. The first step is to work out exactly what you do want from your business. Ensure that you do not fall into the trap of assuming that growth is the only route to success, or that everything you do should be driven only by financial returns.

Defining success

Start by analysing what you want from your business. Of course you want an income, but is that all? Most people want other things, a selection of which is listed below:

- Job satisfaction
- Challenge
- Status
- Variety
- Meeting people
- Helping people
- Being your own boss
- Flexibility
- Freedom.

Ask yourself what is most important to you, and whether your business is delivering it:

- Did it ever deliver it?
- Why has it stopped?
- Was it a realistic expectation in the first place?

Take time over these questions. You may be in a hurry to get to the 'business' bit, but if you do not consciously address your personal motivation, it may sabotage your efforts, and you may not realize until it is too late.

Case study

John had worked in marketing for many years, and when his employer of long standing folded, he decided to move to deepest Somerset in England and set up on his own. He took on a number of his old clients, and found that he was increasingly working remotely on brochures and press releases. Meetings were few and far between, partly because they were unnecessary and partly because even a short meeting was a day's expedition. He was happy to go up to London, which is where most of his clients were, and stay overnight. However, his wife did not like being left alone in the house, and it all became difficult. John lost enthusiasm, got bored with doing the same kind of work, and started to get bad headaches on a regular basis.

An old friend and colleague, Simon, came down to stay for the weekend, and they went out for a drink, just the two of them.

'You don't look well, John,' was Simon's opening comment, when they were settled in the snug with a beer in front of them. John then started to tell Simon how fed up he was, how the work had got boring, how, although he loved the country, he missed the buzz of London and, most of all, he missed the client contact. It was only when he was pouring his heart out to Simon that he realized how important people contact was to him. He had taken it for granted before, and only now, when he was starved of it and suffering the consequences, did he realize it was one of his key motivators.

They discussed the problem, and the solution became obvious. John needed to find some new clients in Bristol, barely half an hour away, and perhaps even consider employment in Bristol, because being surrounded by people was what energized him. Even with clients close to hand, he was not sure it would be enough. In the event, he joined a small partnership in Bristol, and worked two days a week from home. His headaches disappeared, and his energy returned.

If John had seriously analysed what was important to him about his work, he could have saved himself a painful experience. As it was, he could make the change very easily. He had not invested in stock, staff or premises, which could all have made it a much bigger decision.

Another issue to face is whether you have changed. An ex-rock star was recounting when he decided to give up performing. It was the night that he found he was thinking about his laundry during the show! Playing live had been a thrill and a challenge, but now it was less absorbing than a clean shirt. He had moved on, and you too may find that servicing cars is no longer very interesting, or that you are tired of manicuring people's nails.

If this is the case, read Chapter 15 on passion and it will take you through all the steps to finding it; Chapter 21 on commitment will help you to find a new focus.

What do you want from the business?

Assess whether you want new things from the business or just more of the same. If it is something different, it is a question of working out how the business will need to change in order to deliver something fresh. By the end of this process, you will be able to define your personal list of requirements, and you will know what constitutes success in those terms.

Next, we need to look at your business criteria for moving on. Are you happy to take some risks or is financial security paramount? Do you want to go for a big leap or just small steps? Below is a list of business criteria. As with the personal criteria on page 218, list them in order of importance to you so that you can see clearly what is driving your decision making about the future. If you have a business partner, it is vital to do this exercise together. If one of you wants security and the other is impatient to move into the big time you are not going to have an easy ride together, whichever route you take.

- Security
- Risk
- Major growth
- Downsize
- Stability
- More staff
- Lower cost base
- New products/services
- New markets
- Move premises
- Higher profits
- Contribution to charity/community.

This list is not exhaustive; there may be things that really matter to you that are totally specific, like opening an office in Costa Rica or winning a royal crest. Whatever they are, note them down alongside your personal criteria, and then take stock. You may find that some criteria conflict. You may want expansion and a high level of security. If expansion means obtaining major funding, that may not satisfy your need for security. Expansion could mean much more selling for you, when it is the thing that you hate doing. How badly do you want to expand, or are there ways that you could get the selling done by someone else, or expand without raising money?

It is unlikely that you will do a good job of working these things through on your own. If you do not have a business partner or colleague, this is the time when you really need that business buddy before you consider paying for expertise. Do not rush to the detail of costings and projected sales before you have sorted out your broad-brush approach.

If you go too far down the business plan road, you are likely to end up sitting in front of a bank manager or business angel before you have worked out if this is really the right way to go. It is so easy to be driven by the momentum of an expansion programme, and then find that the doubts hit you just as you are about to sign that loan document. By this time you realize you will look stupid if you change your mind, so you sign, and a little voice inside you is telling you that you are not happy. You ignore it, and hope it will go away, but in many cases it will not. You will find you are on what should be an exciting new road, with something holding you back. When you have listened to all your internal 'voices', and found a way forward that meets all your criteria, then you are ready for the next step: creating your vision.

Creating your vision

Your vision will be easy to create because you are now very clear about what you want. Now that you have defined success, all you have to do is to step into the future and experience that success. What will it be like? Take time to examine it with all your senses. When you can see, hear and feel it, you will have all you need to describe your vision. Define it in positive terms, because aiming for a positive gives you a much clearer focus and takes you faster to success.

Making your vision robust

When you have your vision, you can work on turning it into a clear outcome by thoroughly defining and testing it. This process is covered in detail in Chapter 21 ('Defining your outcome'), but it is repeated in summarized form here because it is so vital to your future planning:

- What will I see/hear/feel when I reach my outcome?
- What is the context in which this outcome will be achieved? When, where, who with?

- How will the outcome impact on me, my family, friends and personal life?
- What are the barriers I might face?
- What stops me?
- Is this worth doing compared to staying as I am?
- What internal resources do I need?
- Do I really want this outcome?
- How could this outcome be more compelling?
- What is my first step?

Follow the steps described in Chapter 21 ('Defining your outcome') and, at the end, if you find yourself reluctant to take that first step, go back to the problem questions on the list and deal with them because you have not yet made the right decision.

On the other hand, if all is well, the first step will feel absolutely right. In fact, you might find that you are already taking the first step.

Steps to success

Key questions to ask:

1 Am I really clear about where I want the business to go next?
2 What will that do for me?
3 What will it do for others involved?
4 Is anything holding me back?
5 If so, who can I talk to?
6 What do I need to do to feel 100 per cent right about my future plan?
7 Am I excited by my vision?
8 How do I feel about my first step?

24

making plans

Once you know that your outcome is right for you, and you
have a clear vision of your success, you can invest your efforts
in the detailed planning. If you are raising any kind of funding,
you will need a business plan. Even if no one else is involved,
you will want a plan anyway as part of measuring your success
and of managing the whole process.

What is the plan for?

Before your heart sinks at the thought of preparing a hefty
document, remember that you are preparing this plan for you,
as your action plan, and anything else is secondary to that. Ask
yourself what you want to see in a plan, for example:

- Why am I doing this?
- What is the timeframe for my plan?
- What are my specific goals – revenue and profit
- How do I know that there is a market for my new plan?
- How did I arrive at my sales forecast?
- What are my plans for marketing and selling?
- What investments – in people, stock, premises, marketing,
  equipment, etc. – do I need to make?
- Will I have enough cash during this period?
- If not, do I need to borrow more to fund it?
- How will I pay back any funds I have borrowed?
- How do the risks and threats I face stack up against the
  opportunity?

Business plan headings may look more sophisticated, but they
cover the same topics, and they are all about the future. There
is no need to say much about the past except where it supports
your case, as in sales history, for example. As this is your
document, keep it brief.

The financial section of the plan will take the form of
spreadsheets. If you are happy with them, do a first draft
yourself before you ask someone else to cast an eye over them,
and if you are seeking funds, pay a professional to check them.
If you are not happy with spreadsheets, now is probably a good
time to learn. Doing the spreadsheets yourself enables you to get
to grips with the numbers so that they become yours and you
understand how they work. It may seem like hard work, but it
will be worth it. You can buy spreadsheets which are formatted
to produce cash flow forecasts automatically, for example.

However, if that is really not practical, find yourself a 'man who can', and be sure you understand what they produce! If you start to get lost in a mass of data, go back to your original list of questions to regain your focus.

Business plan outline

Listed below are the key elements of a business plan which you would present to the bank or an investor. If the plan is just for you, skip the presentation frills but keep the core content, that is, the answers to the questions in the section opposite. If your plan is to be submitted to an investor, be sure to read Chapter 26 on funding which has much to say about writing business plans specifically for investors.

1 **Cover page.**
2 **Contents.**
3 **Executive summary** (no more than three pages). Why, what, when and how much.
4 **Objective.** What do you want to do? Achieve sales of x, profit of y.
5 **Funding requirement.** If you want money from the bank or an investor, how much, what for, and for how long?
6 **Mission.** What is your business about? This example gives you an idea of where to start:

   'We install rental gymnasium equipment into companies who care about staff fitness.'

   You might also want to include where you are aiming for in your market, or how you view customer satisfaction or product quality. However, answer this briefly, preferably in a sentence or two, just to give the big picture context to your objective:

   'We offer the highest calibre service to large organizations across the UK, providing the very best equipment.'
7 **The team.** List the key players who will execute the plan, plus any external advisers. Attach CVs where appropriate. Your aim is to inspire confidence that your team has all the credentials it needs to achieve your aim.
8 **The business environment.** Note all the external factors that may affect your plan – trends in consumer spending, decline in manufacturing industry, new safety legislation, etc. You cannot change these, but you can show that you have taken account of them in your plan.

9 **The opportunity**.
- Market analysis
- Sales forecast and how you calculated it.
- Impact on customers – existing and new.
- Assessment of competition – now and in the future.
- Risks in the plan, and how you will deal with them.

A SWOT analysis can be a useful summary here, listing your Strengths and Weaknesses as a company – these are internal – and then itemizing the Opportunities and Threats which you face, which will be external.

Marketing plan – what you will do over the plan period to achieve your goals in some or all of the following:

- Advertising
- Direct selling
- Mailings
- PR
- Sponsorship
- Exhibitions/fairs
- Seminars
- Website
- E-mailing.

Note: There is some overlap between where a business plan stops and a marketing plan starts; many of the 'Opportunity' headings can be covered in the marketing plan. Chapter 25 covers the marketing plan in full.

10 **The financial plan**.
- Profit and loss account for plan period (at least a year, probably longer).
- Cash flow forecast for plan period showing repayment plans completed.
- Projected balance sheet(s) for end of each plan year.

The Appendix gives a complete business plan for Mai Foods, which follows this model, so that you can see how to fill in each section. In Chapter 25, Mai Foods is also used as an illustration to show how the marketing plan is compiled.

When you put your plan together, do three things:

1 Be realistic, not optimistic.
2 Get all the facts right – including your spelling and arithmetic.

3 Include as many facts as you can to justify the non-factual part of your plan – your sales forecast or your cost savings.

Most plans are about selling more, and you may need a complete marketing plan as part of your business plan to justify your sales figures. Much depends on how different your forecast sales are from your existing sales. If you sell 100 items per day in one town in one shop, it is not too big a leap of faith to believe that you could sell 100 items per day in a similar shop in a similar town with similar customers. You would need to demonstrate that similarity, but you do not need the same level of detail as you would if, instead of opening a second shop, you were planning to increase your sales ten-fold through a mail order catalogue. The further away your plan moves from your own tried and tested history, the more evidence of your assumptions you will need, and the more your investors will require to be convinced.

Testing your plan

Now you have drafted your plan, it will need testing before you do anything else. Give it to your business buddy or to a friend or adviser – anyone who knows enough about business to challenge you, and ask them to give you a grilling on all aspects of the document. In addition, you might ask different people to look at different things, ranging from market assumptions to your spelling. If you are applying for major funding, it is worth investing in some professional help to get your plan in the best shape to win investment. Whether you emerge with you plan intact or amended, you will be much more confident about it when it comes to implementation, or to presenting it to others.

Steps to success

Key questions to ask:

1 Who is my business plan for?
2 What are the most critical things that the reader(s) – including me – need to know?
3 Do I really understand all the numbers?
4 Is every aspect of my plan convincing?
5 If not, what more can I do to make it convincing?
6 Who can I choose to be my plan's most vigorous critic?

25

preparing the marketing plan

In this chapter you will learn:
- what information you need
- how to assemble the data
- how to create the marketing plan.

When preparing your marketing plan, which does not have to be a massive document, Chapter 17 will be useful. The document needs to be the right size to answer your basic questions:

- How do I know that there is a market for my new plan?
- How have I arrived at my sales forecast?
- What will I do to make it happen?

What information do you need?

Before you start on your marketing plan, check that you have assembled all the information you need. If you are close to your market, most of it will be in your head. However, if you are going into new markets, some research will be needed on the following topics:

1 Who your customers are – how many you have and their profiles.
2 Who your prospects are – how many you have and their profiles.
3 What your customers are buying from you – their perception of what you offer them – which may not be what you think you are selling!
4 When your customers buy – in what quantity or mix.
5 What your customers would like to buy from you.
6 Factors that might affect your business/customers – PEST analysis:
   a Political/legal developments
   b Economy
   c Social trends
   d Technology.
7 Competitive activity.
8 Your strengths and weaknesses versus the competition.
9 Sales methods and routes to market.
10 Pricing trends and customers' price perceptions.

Assembling the data

Case study
Kim Mai wants to extend her business – Mai foods – which imports Vietnamese food into the UK. She has been doing

everything on a very small scale until now, but business is good, she cannot keep up with demand, and she decides to go for expansion.

Although Kim knows the market is out there, she wants to quantify it – for her own information as much as for anyone else's – and she starts on a research programme, using the topics listed above.

Who your customers are – their numbers and profile

Kim is a wholesaler, supplying restaurants and specialist shops directly, mainly in London. She knows that the end users of her products are both Vietnamese and the British middle classes, who are experimenting far more with all kinds of international cuisine and looking for authentic ingredients.

Who your prospects are – their numbers and profile

Kim researches the market further, and finds that there are restaurants in other major cities, and she identifies where there is a significant concentration of Vietnamese immigrants. She also identifies the places where there is a market for the more adventurous delicatessen.

What your customers are buying from you – their perception of what you offer them

Talking directly to her clients, Kim knows that what they value most of all is that she provides a broad range of completely authentic, good quality products.

When your customers buy – in what quantity or mix

There are certainly lower sales in summer, but otherwise no significant seasonal trends. Kim's customers do buy in annoyingly small quantities, but regularly.

What your customers would like to buy from you

Kim's customers will take any new line she offers. She has trouble sourcing a wide enough range of goods.

Factors that might affect your business/customers – PEST analysis

1 Political/legal developments. Government policy on immigration is relevant, but Kim knows there are sufficient Vietnamese residents in the UK already to provide a much bigger market than the one she is currently addressing.

2 Economy. Kim does not think that an economic downturn would have a major impact on her business, and the current economic trend does not indicate that there is anything to fear in the short term.

3 Social trends. Kim finds that there is an increasing interest in Vietnamese food, and she believes that she will be able to capitalize on the growing UK appetite for new tastes in international cuisine.

4 Technology. Apart from making her business efficient, Kim does not see any technological impact on her plans.

Competitive activity

There are two other importers of Far Eastern food products, including Vietnamese products; neither is a specialist. One sells quality; the other offers cheaper products. Kim is the only importer to take the foods and repackage them under her own brand in the UK. None of the supermarkets stock any Vietnamese products.

Your strengths and weaknesses versus the competition

Kim is a specialist, and she operated in the food products market in Vietnam for five years before she emigrated to the UK. She has a reputation for being knowledgeable and for always providing the real thing. Her current problem is that her operation is too small and she does not have the economies of scale of other importers. They can negotiate better rates for shipping etc. because of the volumes they deal in. However, Kim has personal relationships with the suppliers in Vietnam, and believes she gets good prices.

Sales methods and routes to market

Currently Kim delivers everything by mail or courier. With expansion, she will be able to justify her own delivery van. Both of her competitors deliver direct.

Pricing trends and customers' price perceptions

Of Kim's two competitors, one has a limited range of cheaper products; the other quite a good quality range at high prices. To date, Kim has pitched her pricing slightly below the latter. Where her range extends beyond theirs, she will move to premium pricing and, as she becomes well established, she will move all her products to the premium position, testing responses as she goes.

What is missing from this analysis of the market are the specific numbers, which Kim assembles into a spreadsheet, to build into her business plan (see the Appendix). It details her sales to date, figures for Vietnamese residents in the UK, socio-economic profiles of the UK major cities, etc.

Creating the marketing plan

The next step in the process is to transfer all this data into the marketing plan, and to say what marketing actions you will be taking, which is the promotion plan. We shall continue with the Mai Foods example to illustrate this.

Marketing goals

Kim's marketing goal is to increase her sales by 25 per cent in year 4, and 35 per cent in year 5. She will also include a goal about building her brand, and making it synonymous with authentic, high-quality Vietnamese food products.

Promotion plan

Advertising

Kim will put small advertisements in the publication *Far Eastern Restaurateur* for three months to test the response she gets. She will do the same in the quarterly *Eastern Deli Delight*. She will work hard to get editorial coverage in both, and she knows that advertising can oil the PR wheels, despite many claims by magazines to the contrary.

Costs: £XX per ad in *Far Eastern Restaurateur*, £XX per ad in *Eastern Deli Delight*.

Expected return: one new client for every two advertisements.

Direct selling

Kim's main thrust will be to contact a target list of restaurants and delicatessens directly. She hopes to buy a list cheaply from the two magazines mentioned above, otherwise she will pay her young nephew pocket money to research names, addresses and phone numbers on the Internet. She will try to sell on the phone and, if the prospect looks worthwhile, will go and visit them.

Costs: Price of target list – £XX or payment for research £X.

The other major cost will be in hiring a temp for two days a week for eight weeks in order to help Kim with the administration. In this way, Kim can dedicate her time to selling on those days.

Kim expects to make 30 calls a day, and to convert one in five to a sale, so she plans to win 12 clients per week over eight weeks, increasing her customer base by 30 per cent. She has set herself the target of 100 new clients in six months. If the temp arrangement works well, but her conversion rate is lower, she can extend the timing and still meet her goal.

Mailings

Kim will consider mailing her customer and prospect list when she introduces new lines or has a special offer. For now, she prefers the direct approach in order to build new business.

PR

PR will be the major thrust of Kim's marketing activity. She believes that there is plenty of mileage in Vietnamese recipes with all the women's magazines, as well as with the two specialist Far Eastern publications. She wants to build a reputation as the person to talk to on Vietnamese food and, when she has begun to make inroads with the magazines, she will also target radio and television. Kim has an idea to link Vietnamese festivals with special recipes, and believes that the culture and geography of her country are underexposed in the media, and she can now capitalize on this.

Cost: Kim's time is the only cost here and, since she loves working on recipes, she is happy to do the preparation of press releases in her own time. One of her business advisers has a background in PR, and has given Kim a list of publications to target.

Return: This is a long-term investment in developing her market and her company's reputation. However, if Kim were ever to feature in a TV programme, she knows that this would have an immediate impact on sales through her retailers.

Exhibitions

A number of Kim's delicatessen clients exhibit at the Far Eastern Food fair, and to date she has not invested anything in this show. She may consider sponsoring one or more of her clients to do a special display of her products, and perhaps make up a recipe to offer visitors to the show.

Cost: Kim has budgeted £XX to work with just one client at the show next year.

Return: Kim does not expect to see any immediate return. This is a long-term investment in the Vietnamese food market in general, and her own and her company's profile in particular.

Seminars

One of Kim's more adventurous delicatessens does cookery demonstrations in conjunction with the restaurant next door. Like the exhibition, this could be a longer term development activity, continuing to build on her specialist reputation. Kim will not budget any activity during this growth phase.

Website

Kim's current site is very basic, and she will invest in a more professional look with far more information about Vietnamese food, which will be available to all visitors to her site. She will also set up trade-only pages, so that they can order and she can invoice online. At the moment, this will be useful to only a minority of her customers, but Kim knows that this is the way to go, and she will encourage online transactions whenever she can.

Cost: Budget £XX for website update and addition of trade pages.

Return: General website is a long-term investment. The trade pages will increase operating efficiency as more of her clients use them.

E-mail

Kim may consider email in the future as a way to keep in touch with some of her more computer-literate clients – at the moment e-mail is not a preferred medium of communication for many of them.

Sponsorship

Kim has no plans for this in the short term, but she will work on it as an opportunity to build further PR opportunities for her company, possibly through charities connected with Vietnam, or through some culinary programme.

In summary, Kim is planning a great deal of marketing activity, but in fact she is spending relatively little. Her biggest cost will be to pay the temp while she is doing the selling herself. Kim has tried fitting in sales among her other tasks, and knows it does not work – because it is not urgent, it always goes to the bottom of the pile. She has also considered paying someone else to do the selling, but she has so much knowledge and enthusiasm for Vietnamese food that she finds that once she has begun the call, she enjoys the conversation, even if they do not buy. Her other major expense will be the website, but she knows someone who works from home and charges very reasonable rates.

Kim's marketing plan is an excellent example of intensive marketing activity on a low budget. If she eventually manages to feature on TV, she will have the equivalent of a six- or seven-figure advertising spend – a handsome return for some intensive PR investment of her time.

Steps to success

Key questions to ask:

1 Can I describe what my customers and prospects want from me?
2 How well have I done my research?
3 Where would I rate my sales forecast on the optimistic to realistic scale?
4 Will my analysis of my strengths and weaknesses versus the competition stand up to scrutiny?
5 Do I need any marketing advice?
6 How confident am I that my marketing plan will deliver a measurable return?

26

funding

In this chapter you will learn:
- the success factors in obtaining funding
- about types of funding
- a real investor's viewpoint
- how to convince an investor or lender.

If someone asked you to lend them money for their business, what would you want to know? You would ask yourself questions like this:

- Can I trust them?
- Can they offer me any security?
- How committed are they?
- Do they know what they are doing?
- How believable is their plan?
- How risky is this venture?
- Can they pay me back?

Banks and investors take a similar view, but they come from different angles. The bank will go for low risk and security, whereas the investor will be prepared to take more risk but in return for a permanent piece of the business. Blue Prism is a real life example of how to obtain funding from both.

Case study

Blue Prism is an IT company based in the north of England. It needed to raise money from the bank and from investors. It began as a service company, selling bespoke software to streamline business processes in large organizations such as banks. Blue Prism has five staff, and had been running for three years before it decided that additional funding was required to achieve significant expansion of the business. Normally it would be very difficult for a small company to sell bespoke software to a large one, particularly with a complex sales message. Blue Prism succeeded because it was essentially selling cost savings for a relatively low entry price. It also understands its market well, all of which meant that it was able to start up and trade successfully in a recession, winning a number of blue chip clients.

After a while, Blue Prism realized that much of what it did was repeated for each client, therefore the company decided to create software which would automate the process, so that it would have a product to sell. This product would have the potential to generate far more revenue than the company could generate by selling services.

As the managing director, Alastair Bathgate observed, 'We started out in business with a shot-gun approach, and now we have a sniper rifle. We set off down the R&D [research and development] trail. We made a plan, but we were over-optimistic about the timing, and we realized that we would run out of money before the product was ready. Our original development plans were too ambitious, and we needed far more time than we estimated. Perhaps we also let ourselves believe that we could do it in the time we could afford. We had more or less stopped doing services work, and put all our efforts into the new product, so we had to find funding from somewhere, otherwise we would not have had a business at all.

'I set about finding suitable venture capital companies, and also approached the bank. I would recommend anyone who hasn't raised funds before to take advice from someone who has. I was fortunate in having friends and business contacts who had this experience, so that I did not need to pay for professional advice.

'I started my research using Google, and I considered every kind of finance, including private investors. It took ages to sort out the funding, about three or four months from start to finish, which is probably quite quick in relative terms, but to us it felt like a long time. It was also very time-consuming, and the negotiations took up the majority of my time for that period. I was very careful in choosing investors – I wanted to find the right match for us – people we could really work with, who would add something to the business. I felt that expertise was as important as cash if we were going to aim for growth.

'Venture capital [VC] money is expensive, and we have sold 40 per cent of our company to them, as well as getting a bank loan under the small firms guarantee scheme. We would not have got the bank loan without the VC funding – it completely changed our risk profile – and that is what convinced the bank, who treated it as a standard commercial loan, irrespective of the government guarantee.

'You could say that we applied for funding too late, as we were dangerously close to running out of money, but it probably worked in our favour to leave it as late as we did. There were two reasons for this. The first was that we had an early version of the product to show to the investors, which gives you so much more credibility. The second was that the mood changed in the funding market, so that IT companies were no longer taboo, as they had been for quite a while. We didn't plan to wait, but we can see that the funding process might have taken a lot longer, if we'd started earlier.

'Now we have appointed two non-executive directors, and we are already recruiting four more staff. We appear as a much more credible organization to our clients, because of the venture capital backing. We will essentially be selling the same solution that we have sold for the past three years, but from a more stable base, and with a much better margin for us and better performance for the client. We can also sell the product to other software companies for them to build solutions for their own clients, so our market becomes much bigger, and revenue will no longer be limited by our time.'

Success factors in obtaining funding

Blue Prism was successful in raising funding for the following reasons:

1 Good track record of success in a recession.
2 Very clear goals, based on achievement to date.
3 Predictability of performance – the company will be selling the same solution to the same market but as a product rather than a service.
4 Ability to demonstrate the product.
5 Growth potential highly credible through product sales and through partner product sales.
6 Well written business plan (Alastair has an MBA, as well as a background in finance and marketing).
7 Strong management team.
8 Clear view of what the company wants from an investor.

Where Alastair excelled was in having a very clear vision of what he wanted to achieve, building on the success of his business to date. He had an excellent grasp of the financial structure he was aiming for, and of future target markets. This gave him a very strong case to put to investors, and has put his company on the road to major success in the future.

Types of funding

If your cash is running low for a short period, an overdraft can be the ideal solution. If you want to buy a new vehicle, a bank loan can be a good option. If, like Blue Prism, you want to embark on a major expansion programme, some form of investment is needed, often combined with money from the bank. There are various types of investor: from friends and family to private investors – often called business angels – and corporate investors, primarily venture capital companies.

The big difference with an investor is that you do not need security, and may not have to repay the money they invest. They expect to recover that through dividends and capital growth when they sell their shares. In exchange, they take a percentage of your company, and some level of business control. To attract investors, you normally need to demonstrate a growth rate in excess of 20 per cent, since it is through high capital growth that they make their money.

As Blue Prism discovered, finding the right investor can be time-consuming, and typically it takes between three and nine months to conclude a deal. Investors tend to specialize in particular market sectors and to lend in set price bands – it is important to know how your profile would fit with theirs. In the 'Taking it further' section there are details of where to start looking, and where to go for advice.

The investor's viewpoint

If, like Blue Prism, you are aiming to raise money from investors, your business plan needs to be written with the investor in mind as the target audience. This means putting yourself firmly in their shoes. Mike Cheeseman, a successful businessman who is now a business angel, describes below what he is looking for when he picks up a business plan:

Key data – up front

'I see lots of business plans, and I know what I'm looking for. As an investor, I want to see immediately how much money you want, what you want it for, and what I will get back in return – either as dividend or capital growth when I sell out. Often people hide this information, and are coy about naming the amount. Some never think of telling me how I get my money out.

'Investors operate in different fund brackets – someone who lends in the £10 million to £20 million zone will probably not be interested in lending smaller amounts such as £500,000. For this reason, it's really helpful to see the amount at the beginning of the document, because then you don't waste your time reading something that does not fit your investment profile.'

Mutual assessment

'I evaluate the investment proposition, but I'm just as interested in the people behind it, as they should be in me. This should be a mutual evaluation process, where we are deciding if we can work with each other, as illustrated by Blue Prism. Investors vary in how much interest they take and how much control they want. Sometimes an investor takes a seat on the board and brings welcome expertise. Sometimes they are seen as interfering, and this is why it is so vital to ensure that goals and values match, if investors are planning to take an active part in the business.

'I suggest that writers of business plans need to decide carefully who they send their plans to. First, decide on the criteria for suitable recipients. Here are some considerations:

- The amount of investment required.
- What growth (revenue, profit, cash) profile does the investor require? (For example, VC investment committees often have well-defined financial criteria for investing and it may be possible to find out what these are before submitting a business plan.)
- The level of risk involved.
- Reputation – beware – not all investors are the same. I believe it is essential to check references on any investor, whether an individual or an institution. Sometimes when the need for funds is urgent, it is so easy to miss out this important step. Remember – marry in haste and repent at leisure!
- Terms of investment – for example, what happens if the plan is not achieved?
- What level of job security will there be for the founders?
- Is any aspect of the funding conditional on performance – can future phases of investment be withheld, can initial investment be reclaimed? (Note that there are several 'creative' ways in which investors can achieve this.)'

Realism

'I look for realism in the plan. I'm so used to seeing over-optimistic sales forecasts combined with underestimated costs that I almost make adjustments automatically. Timing is something I pay close attention to. "How long will it take to make the first sale of a new product?" is a question that is often answered far too optimistically, and this can have a disastrous impact on cash flow. I like to see a good safety margin in the sensitivity analysis. This means that instead of showing a variation of three months in sales receipts, the plan shows what happens if you have to wait six months or even nine months for your sale. Of course, you may not want to think so negatively, but it's an excellent test of your plan's resilience.'

Benefits

'I look for a clear description of the value proposition of the product or service. What benefits will it bring to customers, and why will they buy it in preference to the competition? Sometimes this is so obvious to the person writing the plan that they forget to spell it out. Will the initial value proposition still hold good in, say, five years time?'

Target market assessment

'What may not be so obvious is the size of the target market. I like to see good external evidence of the size of the market. I really want the plan to contain good, solid research so I know this isn't an optimistic 'finger in the air' estimate. Nor do I want to be told that you only need to sell to 0.000001 per cent of a huge market to make great sales. You still have to sell something to somebody, even if they are only a tiny percentage. I am particularly sceptical if this is a new sale – either of a new product or to a new market, particularly if it is both a new product and a new market! If you are planning just to do more of the same, then you can estimate from real experience.'

Summary and structure

'I like the plan to be brief and to the point, but it obviously has to cover all the ground, which often means it runs to 30 pages, including the figures. This means that the executive summary has to work really hard, and should not be longer than about three pages. If you genuinely need to include a lot of material – research data, for example – put it into appendices to give the reader the choice of whether and when to read it.'

Illustrations

'I like diagrams and images in a plan, as well as the spreadsheets. If you have a new widget design – then show me with a drawing! If market trends look dramatic, include a graph or something to liven up the text and make it a more memorable document. I read a lot of these, and I generally find more reasons to put them down than to keep on reading them.'

Future changes

'I find that people often make the assumption that the future will be like the present. It won't! This means that you look at how the market will change, what competition might appear, how technology might affect what you do. It is easy to underestimate the competition, and particularly to assume that they will stay the same, while you progress and develop. They will be busy out there too, and your plan needs to recognize this.'

Presentation

'Do not make the mistake of thinking that the plan will speak for itself, especially if you feel it is really solid. The most important aspect of a plan is its owner or owners, and you need to be at least as convincing as your plan. People lend money to people, not to business plans.'

As you are writing your business plan, put yourself in Mike's shoes, and work through his checklist above, to ensure that you really are addressing the investor's concerns.

Relationships

As regards business relationships for funding, you will, as a minimum, have already established a good relationship with your bank manager, and so you will not be asking for money from a stranger. This area is covered fully in Chapter 18 – do not wait until you want, or worse, need something before you make contact with your bank.

Building a good relationship in advance will probably not be possible with a business angel or a venture capital company, so think hard about the following list of questions and how you would best answer them. The next section gives more guidance.

Convincing investors and lenders

Can they trust me?

'Trust me' are words that do not inspire confidence, and no amount of reassurances on your part will work – in fact the more you try, the more the investor may think that you are protesting too much. Building trust has to be done implicitly, by always keeping your promises – something as small as punctuality will count here, and saying when you do not know, or admitting mistakes. The more open you appear, the more likely people will be to trust you.

Can I offer them any security?

This is a question that the bank will want answered, and by security they mean something physical, like a house. How much you should offer them will be a complex decision based on your circumstances, but it would be nice to think that you will not be homeless if things go wrong.

How committed am I?

Here the story of the pig and the chicken illustrate the point: when it comes to breakfast, the chicken is involved, but the pig is committed. If you are not taking any financial risk yourself, and you can walk away unscathed if the plan fails, then any investor will be uncomfortable. On the other hand, they do not need to see you risk everything you possess either.

Do I know what I am doing?

You need to impress any prospective investor with your knowledge of the market, your track record of success to date, and your commitment to this plan, which you will know upside down and back to front. This will be true because you want that information yourself. You were the first person who had to be convinced, and you were the toughest judge.

How believable is my plan?

When they have heard it all, and you have spoken with authority and conviction, there will still come a time when investors say to themselves that a sales forecast is still only a forecast; no matter what solid data it is based on, there is still an element of risk. The contents of your plan and the way that you present it will have a major impact on how much they believe in it.

How risky is this venture?

As with the previous question, risk assessment is crucial and, although you will have done a good job on the plan and its presentation, you may have chosen a high-risk path that does not meet the criteria of certain investors. Be aware of your risk profile from the beginning, especially if you operate in a volatile market – this may affect the sort of funding organizations you choose to approach.

Can I pay them back?

For the bank, this will mean interest and capital, and a close eye on your repayment plan.

An investor, on the other hand, will be looking for very different things – company growth being the primary goal, and getting their money out the eventual aim.

Before you meet a prospective investor or lender, prepare answers to these questions, and any others you can think of, as part of planning the meeting.

Steps to success

Key questions to ask:

1 How convincing is my plan?
2 How convinced am I?
3 What is the best type of funding for my business?
4 What do I want and not want from an investor?
5 What does an investor or lender want from me?
6 What does an investor or lender want from my business?

27

execution

Execution and implementation

There is little to say on this subject because now that you have your funding, or are ready to embark on your plan, there should be nothing holding you back; in fact you will have started right away.

If you have tested your outcome and then your business plan really thoroughly, you will be sure that it is what you want, and sure that you are totally clear on what is needed to get there. If you have any doubts, go back and check your outcome or your plan because doubts at any stage will sabotage your efforts.

Assuming that all is well, think through how you are going to manage this process of change. Obviously your business plan will be your guide, but you may want to set yourself some milestones to ensure that you systematically monitor your progress. This is for your own information, and quite separate from any milestones you may have agreed with investors because, as always, this whole process is for you, their requirements are secondary. With all the resources you need in place, there is no stopping you now!

Business Plan

Executive summary

Mai Foods is a specialist importer of Vietnamese food, established three years ago in West London. As a wholesaler, we import a selection of the best Vietnamese food products, repackage them under our own brand here and sell them to restaurants and retailers – exclusively in London.

After three successful years of trading, we estimate that we have penetrated no more than 50% of the London market, and our research tells us that there are markets in all the major cities in the UK, including Edinburgh, Glasgow, Manchester, Liverpool, Birmingham and Bristol, both for restaurant and delicatessen sales.

In our research document (Appendix A*) we detail both the trade outlets per location, and also the figures for local Vietnamese populations. It is important to note that our products are also purchased by the professional classes of all nationalities, thanks to a growing interest in different international cuisines, and this trend is an important factor in our future marketing plans.

We have reached revenues of £250,000 in our third year, with a gross margin of 43%. We are now seeking a loan of £33,000 in order to achieve revenues of £310,000 in year 4, which represents 25% growth. This funding is required for a full warehouse facility, delivery van, promotional activity, and one additional employee: a driver/packer. The warehouse would enable us to purchase in larger quantities, and thereby achieve the economies in scale of transport costs that is the one price advantage our competitors have over us at the moment, and will give us a slight margin increase.

I set up the business with personal funding of £20,000, and plan to invest all retained profits into this expansion plan, as I take a minimal salary. Since starting up the business, I have managed with only a small overdraft facility, and the historical figures for the past three years in Appendix B [not provided here] will demonstrate how efficiently the business has been run.

As the owner of Mai Foods, I have specialist expertise in the market for Vietnamese food. I have dual Vietnamese/British citizenship, and eight years ago I went to work in my family food business in Vietnam. I spent five years there, with the express intention of building up my expertise and my contacts in order to launch this import business in London.

I do not have any specialist competitors. There are other importers of Far Eastern foods, but they do not specialize, do not have their own brand, nor do they have my expertise or my contacts. Details of the competition, including my analysis of their marketing strategy and campaign history, are given in the marketing plan, together with my specific promotional activities to build the business, which are extensive, but do not involve any major outlay as they focus on direct selling and PR.

The risks in this project would be in the market size estimates, but these are very tightly documented and independently verified. I have had preliminary discussions with prospects in all of the main cities, and have found no difference at all in their needs and interests in this area, so this makes the sales target look quite conservative. Another risk would be any political instability in Vietnam, but the government is now well established and stable. In any case I have produced a contingency plan to deal with this eventuality, involving manufacture outside Vietnam.

Any other risks are around our ability to deliver, and here our track record speaks for itself. We will be selling the same products to existing markets in the same way, but with a more efficient packaging and delivery mechanism.

I believe that I have a solid case for expansion as my sales projections are conservatively based on independently verified data and on our excellent track record of growth to date.

Objective

To expand the business to achieve growth of at least 25% in the next 12 months:

Annual Sales: £310,000
Gross margin: 43%
Net profit before tax: £32,641

Funding requirement

A loan of £33,000, to be repaid over an 18-month period, to fund:

- The leasing of a 75 m² warehouse space for £XXXX/annually. The site is conveniently located to facilitate international shipments.

- The leasing of a packing and labelling machine for approximately £XX/month.
- The purchase of a second-hand delivery van for circa £XXXX.
- The hiring of a driver/packer.

Mission

To achieve market dominance in Vietnamese food products in the UK by becoming the brand recognized and trusted for its authenticity, its wide range, its high quality and its premium prices.

The team

Title: Managing Director
Name: Kim Mai
Qualifications:
- Business degree from the University of London.
- Five years of experience in sales and marketing at family business in Vietnam.
- Excellent financial and management skills.
- Passion for Vietnamese cuisine.

Employees/Agents

Hung Phan – purchasing agent, resident in Vietnam. He has ten years' experience in this field. He negotiates rates and manages supplier and shipper relationships. He is responsible for quality control locally, and he inspects the products before they are shipped to London.

Holly Jones – part-time bookkeeper – also does some order processing.

Thao Vuong – part-time packer.

Eddi Lo is the candidate for the new driver/packer position – well known to us as reliable and hardworking.

Advisers

Jan Saccari, General Manager, Naylor Brown Foods

Jan is responsible for wholesale distribution of fresh foods to the restaurant trade. She is also on the board of the Association of British Food Distributors.

Noel Lyons, Director, Lyons Neil Bray Fordson – media agency

Noel specializes in public and media relations.

Catherine Delai, Kroner Publishing Ltd

Kroner Publishing specializes in food publications of all kinds.

Please note: all advisers participate on a voluntary basis and no fee is charged for their business advice.

Professional services

Slocombe & Partners

This is our company accountant, who not only delivers the figures, but also advises on tax, business structure, profitability and strategic direction.

The business environment

The key factors affecting our business are:

- British economy
- Political stability of Vietnam
- Popularity of Vietnam as a tourist resort – especially for UK visitors
- British immigration policy
- Tastes in international cuisine
- Trends in eating out, and preparing food at home
- Trends towards healthy eating.

Currently we see that all these trends are favourable for business growth. UK immigration policy might have some small impact on the number of Vietnamese coming into the country, but these numbers are negligible now, and our market estimates are all based on the existing Vietnamese populations in the UK.

The research data presented in Appendix A shows that we have a still untapped market across the UK, of local Vietnamese, but also of an increasing number of other consumers, particularly the BC1 group whose interest in cooking exotic dishes at home is growing. Awareness of Vietnamese cuisine is also growing as Vietnam is establishing itself successfully as a tourist destination. People returning from a holiday want to eat in Vietnamese restaurants or cook something themselves.

The opportunity

Appendix A* gives a summary of our company performance to date, and projection for the coming year. From our first year we have shown steady and consistent growth, which is currently running at 25% per annum, and is projected to increase to 35% by the end of year 5.

Revenue projections

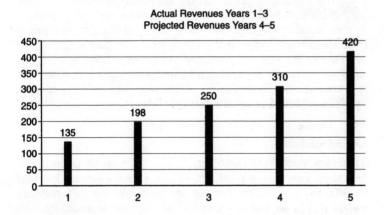

Actual Revenues Years 1–3
Projected Revenues Years 4–5

The size and profile of our target market is detailed fully in Appendix B*, but is briefly summarized here:

Vietnamese populations in major cities outside London:

Brighton: xxxx
Edinburgh xxx, etc.

Numbers of restaurants that offer Vietnamese cuisine:

London: xxxxx
Other major cities: xxxxx

Numbers of delicatessens that offer or could offer Vietnamese food products:

London: xxxxx
Other major cities: xxxxx

Percentage of population interested in ethnic cooking at home:

A study was completed last year of the purchase of ingredients for Chinese food in the north and west London areas, showing that 18% of BC1 consumers purchased these items. We have assumed that this is unrepresentative of consumers across the country, and will be far lower for Vietnamese products, so we have used 2% in our estimates of market potential. Obviously we will not be selling directly to the public, but we will be marketing Vietnamese food to them, and we will use these figures in our sales pitch to delicatessens.

Since our expansion plans involve essentially more of the same, we feel confident that our sales projections are realistic, especially as they assume a significantly lower level of market penetration than we currently have in London. We know our business, our profiling of the size and nature of our target market is solid, our sales ability is proven, as is our business management. There are few uncertainties in the scope of this plan, but we have made a careful assessment of what risks there are.

Competition

There are two other importers of Far Eastern food products, including Vietnamese products; neither is a specialist. One sells quality; the other offers cheaper products. Mai Foods is the only importer to take the foods and repackage them under its own brand in the UK. From our analysis of the competition's promotional activities to date, we have seen nothing aimed at Vietnamese products. Both companies are quite long established with large customer bases. One does regular price promotions, but rarely on Vietnamese products. The other relies heavily on quality of service and broad coverage of all Eastern cuisine, and does very little with price. Neither company offers the breadth of range that Mai has in its specialist field.

None of the supermarkets stock Vietnamese lines, but their listings will be continuously monitored. They are unlikely to introduce an offering without much higher consumer interest, which Mai will be building with its brand. If Mai is successful, a supermarket supply strategy will be prepared.

There are significant barriers to entry for any other new competitor as this market relies on good local contacts in Vietnam and the UK, and expertise in Vietnamese cuisine.

Inventory control

Mai Foods uses the latest inventory control system, specifically designed for wholesalers. The end result is a lower spoilage rate as well as the ability to track popular items. This gives us a competitive advantage over the other two wholesalers in this marketplace.

Seasonal factors

From our sales history we see a slight decline during the summer months, but there is really little variation in purchasing patterns. As most of the products are rice and soy based, there are also no seasonal supply problems.

Import risks

- Political instability in Vietnam (unlikely now) could affect supplies.
- Restrictive duties on food imports from Vietnam (none in prospect) could threaten supply.
- Loss of a key supplier might result in higher prices.
- Shipping problems would cause significant delays in fulfilling orders.
- Currency movement will make Vietnamese products more expensive.
- Change in government regulations on selling food products may force a change in package or product mix.

To avoid these problems, we will:

- Track relevant food legislation and anticipate any changes.
- Ensure that we balance minimizing stock with holding enough to cover any shipping delays.
- Further develop our supplier network in Vietnam.
- Put a contingency plan in place to manufacture outside Vietnam. We have already researched this and identified suppliers in China and Taiwan who could be in production within four months.

• Track relevant economic and political trends to anticipate problems and take early preventative action.

SWOT Summary

Strengths	Weaknesses
Clear business focus	Size versus competition
Efficient operation	New staff
Quality products	Financial exposure
Good reputation	
Good supplier relations	
Good advisers	
Good marketing plan	
Expertise/Passion for Vietnamese food	
Opportunities	**Threats**
Size of market – outside London + further potential in London	Competition – especially pricing
Unexploited market for Vietnamese foods	Import barriers
Opportunity to build a brand	Shipping delays
	Political unrest
	Currency fluctuation

Marketing plan

This section gives full details of our marketing and sales plan for the next 12 months. It is both intensive and highly cost-effective, with the prime focus on direct selling and PR.

Note: the marketing plan appears in Chapter 25 and covers specific plans for the list below:

- Advertising
- Direct selling
- Mailings
- PR
- Exhibitions
- Seminars
- Website
- E-mailing
- Sponsorship.

Financial plan

- Profit and loss account
- Cash flow forecast
- Projected balance sheet.

In these documents we project the expansion plan to the end of year 4, showing the impact on profitability, revenues and cash.

There are also projections to the end of year 5, to show the growth in sales revenue and the full repayment schedule for the loan*.

*In order not to overload the reader with spreadsheets, the year 5 information is not shown in the book, nor are any of the appendices which are referred to in the text.

Happily ever after...

The outcome of this plan was that Mai Foods secured their funding, but in a better form than was suggested in the plan:

- The van was acquired via lease/purchase.

The short-term requirement for £10,000 was in the form of an overdraft, secured against receivables, and the remainder was a loan for 18 months.

This was the cheapest and most effective mix of funding for Mai.

Profit and loss account

PROFIT AND LOSS ACCOUNT

Month	Jan	Feb	Mar	Apr	May	Jun	Jul	Aug	Sep	Oct	Nov	Dec	TOTAL YEAR
Sales	15,000	19,000	25,000	26,000	30,000	30,000	25,000	20,000	25,000	35,000	35,000	25,000	**310,000**
Cost of sales													
Opening stock	14,000	15,000	14,000	13,000	15,000	15,000	13,000	10,000	14,000	20,000	19,000	11,000	**14,000**
Purchases	9,500	9,900	13,200	16,800	17,000	15,000	11,300	15,500	20,200	18,600	11,500	13,000	**171,500**
Total stock	23,500	24,900	27,200	29,800	32,000	30,000	24,300	25,500	34,200	38,600	30,500	24,000	**185,500**
Closing stock	−15,000	−14,000	−13,000	−15,000	−15,000	−13,000	−10,000	−14,000	−20,000	−19,000	−11,000	−10,000	**−10,000**
Stock sold in month	8,500	10,900	14,200	14,800	17,000	17,000	14,300	11,500	14,200	19,600	19,500	14,000	**175,500**
Gross profit	6,500	8,100	10,800	11,200	13,000	13,000	10,700	8,500	10,800	15,400	15,500	11,000	**134,500**
as a %	0.43	0.43	0.43	0.43	0.43	0.43	0.43	0.43	0.43	0.44	0.44	0.44	**0.43**

Expenses	Jan	Feb	Mar	Apr	May	Jun	Jul	Aug	Sep	Oct	Nov	Dec	
Employee costs	1,903	1,903	3,872	3,872	3,872	3,872	3,872	3,872	3,872	3,872	3,872	3,872	42,526
Agent fees	1,200	1,200	1,200	1,200	1,200	1,200	1,200	1,200	1,200	1,200	1,200	1,200	14,400
Premises costs	590	1,875	1,875	1,875	1,875	1,875	1,875	1,875	1,875	1,875	1,875	1,875	21,215
General and office expenses	542	542	542	542	542	542	542	542	542	542	542	542	6,504
Motor expenses	200	200	400	400	400	400	400	400	400	400	400	400	4,400

Advertising and promotion	100	250	600	250	1,000	200	100	100	750	700	100	100	4,250
Legal and professional costs	154	154	154	154	154	154	950	154	154	154	154	154	2,644
Interest	85	95	180	180	180	230	230	230	250	230	200	200	2,290
Depreciation	110	110	235	235	235	235	235	235	235	235	235	235	2,570
Other expenses	80	80	80	80	80	80	80	100	100	100	100	100	1,060
TOTAL	4,964	6,409	9,138	8,788	9,538	8,788	9,484	8,708	9,378	9,308	8,678	8,678	101,859
Net profit before tax	1,536	1,691	1,662	2,412	3,462	4,212	1,216	−208	1,422	6,092	6,822	2,322	32,641
Tax	−460	−507	−498	−723	−1,038	−1,263	−364	63	−426	−1,827	−2,046	−696	−9,785
Net profit after tax	1,076	1,184	1,164	1,689	2,424	2,949	852	−145	996	4,265	4,776	1,626	22,856
Expenses less depreciation	4,854	6,299	8,903	8,553	9,303	8,553	9,249	8,473	9,143	9,073	8,443	8,443	99,289

Jan 2xxx – Dec 2xxx

Cash flow forecast

CASH FLOW FORECAST

Month	Jan	Feb	Mar	Apr	May	Jun	Jul	Aug	Sep	Oct	Nov	Dec	YEAR
Cash inflow													
Collection of receivables	13,000	18,000	19,000	23,000	28,000	27,500	24,000	15,000	20,000	30,000	31,000	18,000	**266,500**
Bank loan	6,500	7,500	3,000	2,000	2,000	1,000		1,000	10,000				**33,000**
Total	19,500	25,500	22,000	25,000	30,000	28,500	24,000	16,000	30,000	30,000	31,000	18,000	**299,500**
Cash outflow													
Repayment of bank loan											11,000	1,000	**12,000**
Paymt of accts payable	12,000	11,000	12,000	14,000	19,000	18,000	9,000	10,000	19,000	18,000	9,000	8,000	**159,000**
Monthly expenses (excluding deprecation)	4,854	6,299	8,903	8,553	9,303	8,553	9,249	8,473	9,143	9,073	8,443	8,443	**99,289**
Drawings	1,500	1,500	1,000	2,000	1,500	1,700	3,000	1,000	1,700	2,000	1,500	2,636	**21,036**
Purchase used vehicle		6,000											**6,000**
Total	18,354	24,799	21,903	24,553	29,803	28,253	21,249	19,473	29,843	29,073	29,943	20,079	**297,325**
Increase/decrease in cash	1,146	701	97	447	197	247	2,751	-3,473	157	927	1,057	-2,079	**2,175**
Opening cash position	411	1,557	2,258	2,355	2,802	2,999	3,246	5,997	2,524	2,681	3,608	4,665	**411**
Closing cash position	1,557	2,258	2,355	2,802	2,999	3,246	5,997	2,524	2,681	3,608	4,665	2,586	**2,586**

Jan 2xxx–Dec 2xxx

Note: VAT is not shown here as Kim keeps a separate VAT account where she puts all VAT collected, and from which she pays VAT due. Depreciation is excluded from expenses, as it is not a cash item.

Projected balance sheet

PROJECTED BALANCE SHEET

Fixed assets

Delivery vehicle	6,000		
Equipment	5,300		
	11,300		
Less: Accumulated depreciation	−3,570		
	7,730	7,730	

Current assets

Cash	2,586		
Accounts receivable	43,500		
Stock	10,000		
	56,086	56,086	56,086

Liabilities

Current liabilities

Bank loan		
(next year's repayment)	13,000	
Accounts payable	9,750	
Income taxes payable	9,785	
	32,535	32,535

> Current assets minus current liabilities

> Current plus fixed assets = total assets

Net current assets	**23,551**	
Total assets		63,816
Total assets less current liabilities		31,281

Long-term liabilities

Bank loan	
(final repayment)	−8000
Net assets	**23,281**

> Total assets less current and long-term liabilities

Represented by:

Proprietor's capital account

Balance brought forward	1,461	
Capital introduced	20,000	
Profit for year	22,856	
	44,317	
Less drawings	21,036	
	23,281	

Balance, carried forward		**23,281**

Dec 31 2xxx

taking it further

There are a million books and websites out there to help the small business – too much information, in fact! Therefore, in this section I offer a small selection of sources of targeted information and guidance.

General business advice

Free advice

An obvious starting place for advice on running your own business is **Business Link** which has many offices in the UK: 'The national network of advice centres for businesses great and small.' They will always 'know a man who can'. Its website is full of useful guides, and very helpfully directs you to specific sources of information: www.businesslink.org

Advice via a membership fee

There are various organizations that you can join that offer advice as part of the membership fee. This might apply to any trade or professional organization relevant to your business.

Chamber of Commerce

Your local Chamber of Commerce will charge a low annual fee – starting at around £100 – and will offer various advice services, including a legal helpline. To find your nearest Chamber of Commerce visit www.chamberonline.co.uk

e-Co

Enterprise Support Partners run an online club for small businesses. You can join for a small – single figure – monthly fee. This will provide you with networking, advice, support and, if you pay a little more, sales opportunities. Examples of the information e-Co provides are working templates to automate your cash flow forecasting, guides to raising funding or checklists for employment contracts. The real benefit is in the community, because you can learn as much from the real experience of the members as from the many e-Co services. This could be the right place to find a really good business buddy. E-co currently has over 2500 members across the UK, some of whom I interviewed for this book, as the club was certainly the most useful and proactive source of information that I found for my research. For further details contact Enterprise Support Partners on 01829 749181 or try out the e-Co at www.e-co.co.uk

Advice for a fee

IBD is the most practical, straight talking and affordable resource that I have found for small businesses. It operates a network of consultants across the country that specialize in small businesses and nothing else. It ensures that all its advisers have real-life experience of running a business. This means that they can roll their sleeves up and help, if you want them to, as well as offering advice. It also means that behind each adviser is a central resource, with expertise in everything from raising funding to avoiding insolvency. IBD will give you a free one-hour business audit, and they are flexible in how and when they charge for their services. If you are looking for paid professional advice, this is a good place to start: www.ibd-uk.com; tel: 0870 755 0890.

For other sources of professional advice, personal recommendation is the best route and, if you draw a blank with your own business network, you can ask Business Link or any organization you belong to for their suggestions.

Two organizations that were helpful to me in writing this book also offer services to small businesses:

Jenner & Co is an accounting company in Buckinghamshire (01908 630230) that specializes in dealing with small businesses. The company have built a reputation for explaining complex matters in simple terms, which is particularly helpful to those just starting up or looking to grow their business. An initial consultation is free of charge. www.jenneraccountants.co.uk

Suttledesign is a small company in Dublin (+353 1 490 9472) that covers all aspects of design, from websites to brochures. You can see their work at www.suttledesign.com

Specific business advice

To some extent, you can look to the same sources for specific advice as you would for general advice, but there are some differences. While you will easily find an employment lawyer or a telemarketing agency, some skills are not so widely known.

For example, if you want a market research consultant, your local chamber of commerce may not have a contact. In this case, you need to find the relevant professional body and work from there. Here, the Internet is invaluable and you will find everything from the Market Research Society to the Government Insolvency Service. Often the Business Link website (www.businesslink.org) will be a good route to finding the right resources. I list some examples here, but the list is endless.

Dismissing staff

The 'Dismissing staff' entry in Business Link (www.businesslink.org) shows the following:

1 A link to the DTI website on fair and unfair dismissal
   www.dti.gov.uk/er/individual/fair-pl714.htm
2 A link to the Employment Tribunals website for details of handling tribunals:
   www.employmenttribunals.gov.uk/default.asp
3 A link to the ACAS code of practice and the ACAS helpline:
   www.acas.org.uk
4 Two checklists for you to assess your company termination and redundancy procedures.
5 A link to the Law Society's website for you to find a specialist local solicitor:
   www.lawsociety.org.uk/choosingandusing/specialise.law

Insolvency

If you type insolvency into the Business Link website (www.businesslink.org) search bar, it brings up a page which gives you the following information:

1 Definition of the two tests for insolvency – insufficient money to pay your debts, or the value of your assets is smaller than the total of your debts.
2 How to do the relevant calculation to check on your own status.
3 Phone numbers for insolvency helplines.

4 The Government Insolvency Service website:
www.insolvency.gov.uk

5 The Law Society site where you can find an insolvency lawyer
who deals with small businesses:
www.lawsociety.org.uk/choosingandusing/helpyourbusiness/
foryourbusiness.law

6 Details of a low-cost computer-based financial training
course, and local workshops on related topics.

Market research

There are several market research websites that have guides and
directories. In particular, the Association for Qualitative
Research has a number of very small organizations as members,
and if you call them they will be happy to help you find the right
one: www.aqr.org.uk; tel: 01480 407227.

There is also the Independent Market Research group, which
has only independent market researchers as members:
www.indepconsultants.org

For the full range of research organizations, go to the Market
Research Society, or the British Market Research Association:
www.mrs.org.uk; www.bmra.org.uk/selectline/login.asp

When looking for a research organization, the first, most
important – and simplest – check is whether it has membership of
the Market Research Society (MRS). This guarantees adherence
to a strict code of conduct and professional standards. The MRS
also offers basic courses for anyone interested in gaining an
overview of market research techniques and their uses.

Investment and funding

Start with the Business Link website (www.businesslink.org),
for a general view. Your options fall into the following
categories:

Banks – not just your own, although this should be a source of
general information on the subject, including government loan
guarantees.

Grants – There are limited UK and EU grants available for
certain types of business ventures – Business Link can advise you
(www.businesslink.org).

Investment

• Private investor – friends, contacts, family. AngelBourse is a
community of private investors that specializes in the small

business arena, and operates in the £100,000 plus investment zone: www.angelbourse.co.uk

- Business angel – Mike Cheeseman, who contributed to the funding section of this book, is a business angel who specializes in the IT and education sectors. Email: mike.cheeseman@btinternet.com
- Venture capital companies – these tend to deal in larger investments – start by looking at www.bvca.co.uk and www.evca.com

Networking

Networking groups exist in many fields. You can use them as business buddies or as a source of leads. It is really useful to get together with people in similar roles who have faced similar problems to you, for example. This may not necessarily mean they are in your particular sector, so it may take you time to find the right group for you, but there are lots of them out there.

The best-known and established networking groups are BRE and BNI. They have a long track record in this field, and generally work on the basis that you must attend meetings very regularly, and they do not normally allow competitors in the same group. However, there are many local groups, so this should not be an issue.

BRE is the Business Referral Exchange – www.brenet.co.uk

BNI is Business Network Inc. – www.bni-europe.com

Whatever information you need, with a combination of the sources listed here and the Internet, you will find it!

index